CONCEPT
OF
FREEDOM

A SOCIO – THEOLOGICAL INQUIRY

ANSELM KENTUS CHIJIOKE EKE, MSP (PhD)

authorHOUSE

AuthorHouse™
1663 Liberty Drive
Bloomington, IN 47403
www.authorhouse.com
Phone: 833-262-8899

Published by AuthorHouse 08/18/2020

ISBN: 978-1-7283-7074-3 (sc)
ISBN: 978-1-7283-7073-6 (e)

Library of Congress Control Number: 2020915895

Print information available on the last page.

This book is printed on acid-free paper.

ACKNOWLEDGEMENT

I am immensely grateful to almighty God for his grace which has enabled me to realize this project. In the course of my ministry and studies, many friends (so numerous to mention names here), parishioners and family members have served as pillars of support and encouragement for me in so many different ways; I want to say thank you to all of you for your generosity and kindness. I am also indebted to those who contributed helpful ideas as I was putting this work together and challenged me to put this work into the book form it has today. To all the teachers who have guided me in my studies, many thanks. Lastly, I will like to single out and thank Dr. John Henry Morgan, who diligently proofed this work and approved it.

To all of you, I pray God's abundant blessing upon you and your families.

TO GOD ALONE BE THE GLORY

DEDICATION

This work is dedicated to the loving memory of my late parents
Emmanuel and Marcillina Eke
Who instilled in me the love for learning and taught
me that freedom can only be found in Christ.

Contents

Introduction...xiii

1. What is Freedom...1
   I.   Relationship between liberty and freedom.........................1
   II. Sphere of Freedom..5
        a. Freedom of Speech:...6
        b. Freedom of Assembly: 11
        c. Freedom of Religion: 15
        d. Freedom to Petition the Government:.........................20
        e. Freedom of the Press..25
   III. Limits to our freedom 29

2. Freedom and Existentialism 33
   I.   The Existentialist thinking..33
   II.   The man Viktor Frankl 34
   III. What is Freedom in Existentialism? 41
   IV.   Concept of freedom in atheistic existentialism 43
   V.   Jean Paul Sartre...44
   VI.   Subjectivism at the root of freedom..............................48
   VII. The Hole 52
   VIII. Meaning and Values in Sartre.......................................55

3. The Concept of Freedom in Moral Theology 59

   I.   The two concepts 59

   II.   What is Freedom of Indifference? 61

      a. Destruction and Division: 63

      b. Nominalism and Protestantism: 64

      c. Destroy in order to build: 65

      d. Freedom of Indifference and Scripture: 66

      e. Freedom of indifference and the autonomy project: 68

   III.   Freedom for Excellence: 70

      a. Freedom for excellence and Discipline: 71

      b. Freedom for excellence is a freedom to serve: 72

      c. Freedom for excellence and Grace: 73

4. Freedom and Grace 77

   I.   Exclusive Alternatives? 77

   II.   The Providential Love of God 78

   III.   Powers and limitations of fallen nature 81

   IV.   Sanctifying Grace 84

   V.   Sharing the Divine Life 86

   VI.   Actual grace and Free will 88

   VII.   Efficacious Grace and Supernatural Merit 91

5. Freedom in Christ 95

   I.   The existential question 95

   II.   Meaning of our existence 98

   III.   Self understanding 101

   IV.   Authentic Freedom 103

   V.   Called to freedom 104

   VI.   The implication of the freedom we have in Christ

      Jesus 107

6. Freedom from Militating Conditions 112

    I.   Freedom from Sin 113

    II.   The Meaning of Suffering 118

    III. Freedom from the fear of Death 122

    IV. Resurrection of the Body 128

    V.   Freedom in relation to our final destiny and
        Christian living 132

7. Freedom is an All Inclusive Phenomenom 136

    I.   Freedom is found only in relationship with others 136

    II.   No man is an island 140

    III. Freedom is the Essence of Existence 142

    IV. Freedom calls us to a reverence for all life 145

Introduction

Just as it is in the nature of human beings to seek happiness so it does belong to their nature to seek freedom and to act freely. Pinckaers underlined the importance of freedom to humans when he wrote: "Freedom is at the heart of our existence."[1] And it is true, for events in life have shown how much people resist any attempt to restrict their freedom. Yes, we are always seeking freedom, be it freedom from something (sometimes freedom from laws and obligations) or freedom to do something. One of the great fathers of the American Revolution, Patrick Henry is quoted to have said so many years ago, "Forbid it, Almighty God! I know not what course others may take; but as for me, give me liberty or give me death!"[2] This is an indication of how much value he had placed on freedom. It was for freedom that the Pilgrims left Europe to settle in the 'new world' we know today as the United States of America – and how much they had to undergo to arrive at this freedom.

We live in a world today where freedom is readily on people's lips. Freedom is used to explain whatever we believe and do. Sociologists will speak of the freedom people have in living out their cultural heritage and protecting same from others seeking to obliterate their

---

[1] *Pinckaers Servais, OP- The Sources of Christian Ethics P.238*

[2] *Give Me Liberty Or Give Me Death: Speech given by Patrick Henry, March 23, 1775.*

cultures. We will hear again and again about the economic freedom that should exist, with the mention of free trade and its related programs. Environmentalists are not left out in the fight for freedom for the environment including all animals and plants. Political activists will do everything to ensure that peoples in the different parts of the world are ruled by democratic leaders freely elected by the people. Of course there are still militants who claim to be fighting for freedom, and we know how most of these go at the end of the day. What about the cry for religious freedom that rings out every day in every part of the universe? And all these are legitimate claims and aspirations; they require our attention.

Unfortunately though, there are many who equate freedom with license to do what they want and they end up causing harm to themselves and others in society. One person jokingly said, 'Absolute freedom is being able to do what you please without considering anyone except your spouse and your kids, the company and the boss, neighbors and friends, the police and the government, the doctor and the church.' At the end of the day, the question will be asked, 'when people say that they want freedom what do they really mean?' We might ask further, what really is freedom? From my observations I have come to the conclusion that there are false and true freedoms; but how can we differentiate these? How do we know each when we come across them? I mean, what are the distinctive marks of true freedom and false freedom? And if it is not true freedom in the first place, why do we allow it to go by the name of freedom? Is there a place where true freedom could be found?

Freedom comes with it a level of responsibility; it places a reasonable obligation on the individual. Freedom ought to make the individual humble enough to know and accept his/her place in the order of things. It helps one to appreciate one's humanity and also to recognize one's capabilities and limitations. Freedom is a gift from God with which the individual ought to enter into a relationship with the Creator; it should not be a reason to abandon the Creator. I am convinced that the proper use of freedom will surely make the world a better place and bring glory to God who is the source and summit of our freedom and ultimately of our existence.

I do not pretend to have the answers to the many questions that I have already raised neither do I lay any claim to having the intention to exhaust all the questions that could be posed in relation to the issue of freedom. I am simply setting out on a journey of exploration of freedom and I am hoping that by the end of the journey I would have been able to arrive at some point of clarity to myself and hopefully others who would read this work as to what constitutes true freedom and in whom this true freedom could be found. I will sure be operating from my Christian background and hope that at the end I would have been able to prove like St. John Paul II once said: "Freedom consists not in doing what we like, but in having the right to do what is right."[3]

---

[3] *Homily of his holiness John Paul II Oriole Park at Camden Yards, Baltimore Sunday, 8 October 1995*

CHAPTER 1

WHAT IS FREEDOM

I.   Relationship between liberty and freedom

This is one of those terms that people tend to define according to their subjective perceptions. It is rather easier to speak of the nature or notion of freedom than to define it. However after consulting several authors, be they philosophers or theologians, I am inclined to deduce that 'Freedom is the capacity to decide what is good by oneself and not through external constraint.' In everyday speech, it is common to hear the term freedom used in place of liberty and vice versa. According to the Oxford Dictionary, Freedom is 'the power or right to act, speak, or think as one wants.' The same dictionary defines Liberty as 'the state of being free within society from oppressive restrictions imposed by authority on one's behavior or political views.' As a way of clarification, I intend to use the words 'freedom' and 'liberty' interchangeably in the course of this book. I do recognize the fact that there is a possible stretch here, yet it would seem to serve my purpose well to be free enough to use any of these words as I choose. Furthermore the various sources consulted in the course of this research do not seem to make an obvious and absolute distinction between the two words, without prejudice to the already noted difference indicated by the dictionary definition. In fact the only noticeable difference highlighted by some scholars is that of etymology i.e. the fact that freedom has a Saxon origin, while liberty has a French origin; and how insignificant that can be compared to the sense they both make and the importance to which they are held in our world today.

One is said to be free when one is able to choose to do a thing or not do a particular thing. To be free is to be able to choose and to want to choose according to one's conscience. In all we can conveniently say that freedom means choice, and choice entails deciding how to fulfill one's sense of and obligation to self and responsibility. The discussion is still going on as to whether we should speak of freedom in relation to the ability of one doing what he likes or in the ability of one doing what he ought. And whichever way one chooses to speak of freedom makes a lot of difference as to the definition one gives to freedom and how one acts out one's freedom. In this regard the contribution of Isaiah Berlin in his book (Two concepts of Liberty), is monumental. In the article he introduced the idea of positive and negative freedom, an idea I intend to deal with later on in this book. He posited, among many other ideas, that "Positive freedom therefore is less about what individuals are forbidden from doing, and more about what individuals can do to reach their full human potential. Under a state of positive freedom "I wish, above all, to be conscious of myself as a thinking, willing, active being, bearing responsibility for my choices and able to explain them by references to my own ideas and purposes"[4].

According to Law School Prof. Butler Shaffer (in an article posted on the internet on July 22, 2011 by Geoff) "Freedom is your individual ability to do what you want with your time, believe

---

[4] *Berlin, Isaiah. "Two Concepts of Liberty." In Four Essays on Liberty, PP 118-172.*

what you want, think what you want. Freedom is in your core being and cannot be taken away, even by most totalitarian governments, although they may try". Following this definition of freedom, one can conveniently conclude that freedom belongs to an individual just for being born into the world. It is a God-given right of every individual. No wonder the right to freedom/liberty was included in the preamble of the Declaration of Independence of the United States of America, "We hold these truths to be self-evident, that all men are created equal, that they are endowed by their Creator with certain unalienable Rights, that among these are Life, Liberty and the pursuit of Happiness." Freedom has its source and origin from the creator of the universe; to be alive is synonymous to being free. One cannot be said to be fully alive unless one has freedom.

The great philosopher John Locke wrote about freedom, "All men are naturally in a state of perfect freedom to order their actions, and dispose of their possessions and persons as they think fit, within the bounds of the law of Nature, without asking leave or depending upon the will of any other man."[5] Locke, by this assertion, creates a situation in which every individual can afford to live by themselves and care less about what happens to the rest of humanity. The individual owes no responsibility to the community; an assertion he was later to reverse because he realized that it was not possible in the real world for each person to secure his or her own liberty. I believe that our freedom, though natural to every individual, is yet related to the community. While the question still goes on as to whether freedom should consist in one's ability to do what one likes with what one has or one's responsibility to do what one ought to do, we should all recognize that it is something we owe to ourselves and to

---

[5] *Today's Moral Issues, P. 280*

each other – to be free. As the great Martin Luther King observed, "No one is free until all are free".

In the thought of Thomas Hobbes, freedom is that unhindered right an individual has to order the cause of his existence. Thus a human is free in so far as there are no obstacles from outside his nature to the power of his own will or motivation to cause the actions willed or motivated. As Hobbes puts it: "Liberty is the absence of all impediments to action that are not contained in the nature, and in the intrinsic quality of the agent"[6]. The implication of this is that each individual should do everything within his power to remove any obstacle on his way in order to enjoy this liberty. Interestingly, Hobbes agrees that the way to the realization of this liberty is by one being prepared to give to others the same amount of liberty that one wants for oneself. As he puts it, "That a man be willing, when others are so too, as far forth as for peace and defense of himself he shall think it necessary, to lay down this right to all things; and be contented with so much liberty against other men, as he would allow other men against himself".[7] This is akin to the 'Golden rule'.

However Hobbes continued to argue that there was always a difference between right to liberty and an obligation to do everything in order to enjoy liberty; a distinction he was keen to make because of the way his thoughts were being interpreted by others. For him right and law are not one and the same thing; they are different, as he explained, "For though they that speak of this subject used to confound *jus*, and *lex*, right and law; yet they ought to be distinguished, because right, consists in liberty to do or to forbear, whereas law determines and binds to one of them: so that law and right differ as much as obligation and liberty, which in one and the

---

[6] *Hobbes, Thomas (1656) –The Questions Concerning Liberty, P. 285*

[7] *Thomas Hobbes, BrainyQuote.com. Retrieved July 8, 2015, from BrainyQuote.com*

same matter are inconsistent"[8]. This only strengthens his original argument that it was within one's liberty to give up certain rights to another in order that one might fully enjoy one's liberty; if he were forced by law to give up that right, then he would not be said to have freedom. For him law/obligation restricts liberty and consequently is to be considered an enemy of liberty.

From the foregoing, we are in a position to conclude that freedom is our natural right, a right that is handed down (should be handed down) from one generation to another. Edmund Burke expertly articulated this point, "You will observe that from the Magna Carta to the Declaration of Right it has been the uniform policy of our constitution to claim and assert our liberties as an entailed inheritance derived to us from our forefathers, and to be transmitted to our posterity"[9] It shall therefore constitute a failure on the part of any generation if these liberties were lost. We must each fight for our individual freedom and enjoy it without forgetting, however, that we owe it a duty to succeeding generations to preserve liberty. This is the case for freedom being both a right to choose what I want and an obligation for me to do what I ought for the good of the human society.

II.   Sphere of Freedom

There are appropriate areas in which an individual should be allowed to express his or her freedom. Interestingly, the First Amendment to the Constitutions of the United States of America listed five major freedoms which every citizen is entitled to: "Congress shall make no law respecting an establishment of religion, or prohibiting

---

[8] *Today's Moral Issues, P. 278*
[9] *Ibid. P.142*

the free exercise thereof; or abridging the freedom of speech, or of the press; or the right of the people peaceably to assemble, and to petition the Government for a redress of grievances."[10] From this we read that the First Amendment clearly recognized five different types of freedom and they include speech, religion, assembly, press and right to petition the government. I do subscribe to these freedoms and hope that every individual on the face of the earth could enjoy these freedoms. But unfortunately we know there are still a vast majority of human beings to whom these freedoms are unaffordable luxuries. These liberties and even much more are highlighted in an article by John Stuart Mill under the caption of 'the Sphere of Liberty'[11]. For the purpose of this project, I will like to briefly discuss the freedoms granted by the First Amendment namely: Freedom of speech, freedom of religion, freedom of assembly, freedom of the press and freedom to Petition the government.

a. Freedom of Speech:

According to the New World Encyclopedia, "Freedom of speech is the ability to speak without censorship or limitation. Also called freedom of expression, it refers not only to verbal speech but any act of communicating information or ideas, including publications, broadcasting, art, advertising, film, and the Internet. Freedom of speech and freedom of expression are closely related to the concepts of freedom of thought and conscience"[12]. Most democracies in the world offer this freedom and make a strong effort to defend it.

---

[10] *"http://law.jrank.org/pages/6909/First-Amendment.html">First Amendment - Freedom Of Speech, Freedom Of The Press, Freedom Of Religion.*

[11] *Ibid. P147*

[12] *"Freedom of Speech." New World Encyclopedia, 16 Nov 2013, retrieved on 13 Jul 2015,*

The lack of this freedom is one of the distinguishing features of totalitarian and communist regimes. It is to this latter danger that Franklin implied when he wrote, "Whoever would overthrow the liberty of a nation must begin by subduing the freeness of speech."[13] I reckon that it is a very important aspect of human freedom and when judiciously applied, is good both for the individual and the society. Any attempt to prevent one from voicing one's opinion does a disservice to everybody involved, as John Stuart Mill observed, "the peculiar evil of silencing the expression of an opinion is that it is robbing the human race, posterity as well as the existing generation – those who dissent from the opinion, still more than those who hold it."[14] In other words, the practice of freedom of speech makes for a richer exchange of ideas in society, sharpening and clarification of perspectives.

In discussing freedom of speech there are always the two extremes to watch: on the one end we have to realize that allowing limitless freedom of speech could lead to harm of other peoples' good name and disruption of peace and order in society; yet on the other end, placing limits to the individual's freedom of speech is most of the time the beginning of the rule of tyranny and would eventually lead to other restrictions of a people's freedom. It is in consideration of this reality that there have been some scholars who thought freedom of speech does not really exist. For example Stanley Fish argues that speech is never really free; all defenses of freedom of speech make exceptions. He has detailed his position in a well written book called *"There is no such thing as free speech"*. For him "free speech in short, is not an independent value but a political prize"[15] There is always

---

[13] *Benjamin Franklin, Silence Dogood, the Busy-body and Early Writings*
[14] *Today's Moral Issues, P. 148*
[15] *Stanley Fish, There's No Such Thing as Free Speech…and it's a good thing too, P.102.*

a condition and a perspective involved in speaking of freedom of speech.

In the person of John Stuart Mill we have one of the staunchest defenders of freedom of speech. He wrote extensively on this subject matter in his book *"On Liberty"*. There he argued that such liberty (freedom of speech) should exist with every subject matter so that we have "absolute freedom of opinion and sentiment on all subjects, practical or speculative, scientific, moral or theological"[16]. Mill claims that the fullest liberty of expression is required to push our arguments to their logical limits, rather than the limits of social embarrassment. Such liberty of expression is necessary, he suggests, for the dignity of persons. Not even on the assumption of the fact that an individual's opinion may be wrong, should such opinion be silenced. Mill argued that each person's right to their freedom of opinion should be respected, a position that was collaborated by Evelyn Beatrice Hall under the pseudo name, S.G. Tallentyre, when she wrote, "I disapprove of what you say, but I will defend to the death your right to say it."[17]

In history we have had some very high profile cases of the extent of freedom of speech/expression that should be permissible in civil society. The case of Rushdie Salman readily comes to mind when he published the *'Satanic Verses'* which contained in it ideas the Muslims felt were blasphemous against Prophet Mohammed. The carnage the publication caused around the world is well documented. But author Salman Rushdie had asked the question: "What is freedom of expression?" He insisted that "Without the freedom to offend, it ceases to exist." Ben Wizner (director of the American Civil Liberties Union's Speech, Privacy & Technology Project), may not have fully

---

[16] *John Stuart Mill, On Liberty, P.11*

[17] *The Friends of Voltaire by S.G. Tallentyre*

agreed with Rushdie, but he did however think provocative free speech should be allowed as he wrote, "A society in which provocative speech could be punished would be a society without controversial politics, or art, or ideas. It would be a society in which citizens feared expressing dissident thoughts. In short, it would be a society wholly alien to America's founders who, after all, had some pretty provocative ideas of their own"[18]. Several other scholars have lent their support to this view as Jonathan Rauch wrote, "It is not good to offend people, but it is necessary. A no –offense society is a no – knowledge society"[19] Elsewhere Alan Dershowitz said: "Freedom of speech means freedom for those who you despise, and freedom to express the most despicable views. It also means that the government cannot pick and choose which expressions to authorize and which to prevent"[20].

But I am afraid that if we let things go this way, things can get very nasty for society and everyone involved. It should be made abundantly clear that nobody or authority should be in the business of stopping free speech, rather as Jonathan Rauch coined it, "We don't want to block criticism and inquiry, just hate and intimidation"[21] I believe that good sense of judgment must be allowed to prevail in the application of the right to freedom of expression. No one should be given that full liberty to say whatever they want even when it is prone to inciting trouble and harming other peoples' good names. There must be some way of checking and reining in excesses. Pope Francis did agree with my fears when he was asked on his way to Philippine

---

[18] *Statement by ACLU published on PBS website, retrieved on 7/14/15*

[19] *Today's Moral Issues, P. 222*

[20] *Alan Dershowitz." BrainyQuote.com. 14 July 2015. http://www.brainyquote.com/ quotes/quotes*

[21] *Today's Moral Issues, P. 223*

on January 14, 2015 to react on the attack that killed 12 people at the offices of Charlie Hebdo after the magazine outlet was targeted because it had printed depictions of the prophet Muhammad. He responded, "One cannot provoke, one cannot insult other people's faith, and one cannot make fun of faith. There is a limit. Every religion has its dignity ... in freedom of expression there are limits." The Vatican Press office was to later clarify that the Pope's statement did not however justify the attacks on Charlie Hebdo, but rather was emphasizing the fact that there were limits to freedom of expression.

Thankfully Mill, the great defender of freedom of speech, did agree that there was a time when freedom of speech could be limited. This he discussed under his now very famous 'Harm Principle'. In this he does agree with most scholars who have argued that there was always the necessity in every society to have limits to our freedom of speech. Contained in his submission for the restriction of freedom of speech was this understanding: "To justify that (restriction of an individual's right of freedom of speech) the conduct from which it is desired to deter him must be calculated to produce evil to someone else"[22] And only this (preventing harm to the other person), constitutes a valid reason for the restriction of freedom of speech; not because it will make the particular individual appear good in society or even accord him/her any great acclaim among the elite of society. It is under this condition that we class the issue of censorship which has been proposed as necessary at certain times with regard to a certain group of persons. Plato had asked rhetorically, "And shall we just carelessly allow children to hear any casual tales which may be devised by casual persons, and to receive into their minds ideas for the most part the very opposite of those which we should wish them

---

[22] *Today's Moral Issues P.146*

to have when they are grown up?"[23] His answer was no, 'we cannot' and so do I respond.

There is the need to qualify our right to freedom of speech; this is the qualification that has come from no other than Albert Einstein when he wrote, "So long as they don't get violent, I want to let everyone say what they wish, for I myself have always said exactly what pleased me". It is that qualification, 'so long as they don't get violent' that makes all the difference in the application of this liberty under discussion. This position of Mill, Einstein and many others is my preferred position on the issue of freedom of speech: Each person should be free enough to voice their opinion so long as they do not incite violence and do no harm to others. Even as we understand the Fourteenth Amendment as limiting the ability of the government to make laws limiting free speech, but to spread defamatory statements, calumnies and obscenity in my judgment would be inappropriate and ordinarily should not receive protection under the freedom of speech act.

b. Freedom of Assembly:

According to the American Heritage New Dictionary of Cultural Literacy, freedom of assembly is "The right to hold public meetings and form associations without interference by the government". The Thesaurus Dictionary defined freedom of assembly as "the right to peaceably assemble and to petition the government for redress of grievances". This very right which is always qualified as the right to peaceful assembly is also guaranteed by the First Amendment to the Constitution of the United States of America. It was included in the United Nations' Universal Declaration of Human Rights in 1948,

---

[23] *Ibid. P. 132*

Article 20 of which states: "Everyone has the right to freedom of peaceful assembly and association."[24] The understanding regarding this right is that people should be free to gather for peaceful purposes both in public places and also in their private homes unrestricted by government authorities. Persons who are of full age, and not being deceived or forced to gather, should be free to do so under the provisions of the freedom of assembly. The issue of full age is very important in any consideration about freedom of assembly, for the state has right to determine that anyone under the age 18 or thereabout, depending on a particular state and the nature of the assembly in question, could be refused the freedom to gather or form an association.

However, it is important to underline that like many other freedoms, freedom of assembly is not an absolute right and therefore it is required that gatherings in public places, especially for protests, demonstrations, large rallies and parades should receive police clearance, and this strictly is for the maintenance of public order. It also means that the rightful authorities can legitimately turn down requests for the gathering of people that it rightly judges as likely to cause public disorder, might intervene if members of a particular group are shouting, using obscenities, or arguing with or threatening those who oppose them. Rightful authorities can also disband unauthorized gatherings of people even when no disorder is caused by such gatherings. In general authorities may restrict peoples' right to freedom of assembly to protect national security or public safety, prevent disorder or crime, and protect health or morals and/or to protect the rights and freedoms of other people. Unfortunately, there have been times when authorities have abused this power of restriction

---

[24] *Freedom of Assembly. (2013, November 15) New World Encyclopedia, retrieved July 15, 2015*

as would happen in totalitarian regimes or even in Islamic countries where governments are less tolerant to different political, ideological or cultural opinions. And wherever this happens, individuals and society as a whole suffer.

In an article I already cited above from the New World Encyclopedia, the author so well nuanced the idea and importance of freedom of assembly that I would want to cite him verbatim here: "Freedom of assembly is generally recognized as one of the foundations of a democratic nation. Protecting this right is considered crucial for creating an open and tolerant society, in which different and often competing groups live together in a pluralistic environment. Freedom of assembly is also crucial to the development and expression of culture, as well as in the preservation of minority identities. The right to freedom of assembly, however, is not absolute, but must be balanced against the need to protect other rights and needs. Thus, only peaceful assemblies are generally protected. On the other hand, peaceful assemblies that express offensive political messages or "heretical" religious ideas are generally protected under international law. For example, the Organization for Security and Cooperation in Europe (OSCE) interprets the "peaceful" to include "conduct that may annoy or give offense to persons opposed to the ideas or claims that a particular assembly is promoting."[25]

Freedom of assembly is so closely linked to Freedom of Association which has been defined "as the right of people to meet together to further their common goals. Furthering their goals might include such things as organizing their efforts, marching, picketing or gathering in public places"[26]. It also includes the right of individuals

---

[25] *Ibid.*

[26] *revolutionary-war-and-beyond.com/freedom-of-assembly- retrieved on July15, 2015*

to meet freely with other individuals with the goal of forming clubs or societies without any restrictions from the authorities. This is where trade unions come in, but care has to be taken to ensure that targeted groups or individuals are not coerced into joining the unions against their will. Coercing individuals to join trade unions effectively means trampling on their freedom of association rights.

It is true that freedom of association understandably is linked to freedom of assembly which is a fundamental human right, however legislations surrounding the freedom of association would slightly vary from that governing freedom of assembly. This is especially so when we get into the territory of Trade Unions, because governments have to ensure that no group of individuals would be allowed so much power and freedom to hold goods and services meant for the good of society to hostage especially through organized strikes. In a well written document detailing the discussion that went on with regard to the status of strikes in the International Covenant on Civil and Political Rights and the International Covenant on Economic, Social and Cultural Rights, the submission was, "the fact that the International Covenant on Civil and Political Rights does not similarly provide expressly for the right to strike in article 22, paragraph 1, shows that this right is not included in the scope of this article, while it enjoys protection under the procedures and mechanisms of the International Covenant on Economic, Social and Cultural rights subject to the specific restrictions mentioned in article 8 of that instrument"[27]. Yes people have the right to form and join trade unions for the promotion and protection of their economic and social interests, yet the general good of society takes prominence in

---

[27] *bayefsky.com/themes/association_trade_jurisprudence.pdf*

pursuing this right especially when the question of the right to strike comes up.

While we are discussing freedom of association, it will be relevant to examine the question of gangs and its relationship to the freedom of association act. To come to a very clear legal and concise definition of gang is not always very easy since their constitutions vary in nature, but I will take as a working definition that was given to it by the state of Alabama in the U.S.A which states: "Any combination, confederation, alliance, network, conspiracy, understanding, or similar arrangement in law or in fact, of three or more persons that, through its membership or through the agency of any member, engages in a course or pattern of criminal activity." Ala. Code § 13A-6-26 (2002). Following our earlier established basis that such groups and societies should be geared towards peaceful agenda, it does appear to me that violent gangs would not ordinarily be covered under the freedom of association act. Gangs which so often are involved in drugs and other violent activities in society constitute a definite nuisance to public order and security and should not be allowed to hide under the freedom of association label. Fortunately courts in the US, including the Supreme Court, have at various times granted the relevant authorities the powers to regulate the activities of these gangs for the sake of public order. And I do not consider these regulations as interfering with the rights of the gang members to free association especially as their associations are geared towards violent and illegal activities.

c. Freedom of Religion:

By their very nature as humans, endowed with reason and freewill, every man and woman has the right to seek the truth, especially religious truth and when found should be free to live according to that truth. James Madison reflecting on the idea of freedom of religion had said "Because we hold it for a fundamental and undeniable truth, "that Religion or the duty which we owe to our Creator and the manner of discharging it, can be directed only by reason and conviction, not by force or violence. The Religion then of every man must be left to the conviction and conscience of every man: and it is the right of every man to exercise it as these may dictate"[28].

Religious freedom is no different from our general understanding of freedom/liberty, and this is why we call it a right. It is simply put allowing an individual to live according to his conscience and follow the dictates of his heart especially in matters regarding to God both privately and in the public arena. It means that it does not belong to the government to establish any religion or declare one religion as a state religion. This also implies that every individual should be free not to choose any particular religion and to deny the existence of God. The Universal Declaration of Human Rights adopted by the United Nations General Assembly on December 10, 1948, (Article 18) defines freedom of religion and belief as follows: "Everyone has the right to freedom of thought, conscience and religion; this right includes the freedom to change his religion or belief, and freedom, either alone or in community with others and in public or private, to manifest his religion or belief in teaching, practice, worship, and observance"[29]. This right is based on the inalienable dignity of the individual as a human person. Every individual should be free to choose who, when and how to worship unhindered by any government or any other authority, including one's employers.

---

[28] *James Madison, A Memorial and Remonstrate (1785), excerpt from the book, 'We Still Hold these Truths'*

[29] *Freedom of religion. (2013, November 15). New World Encyclopedia, Retrieved July 17, 2015*

Thomas Pazhayampallil has described it thus: "Religious freedom then means immunity for a man from being forced to act against his beliefs and immunity from coercion which restrains a man from acting in accordance with his conscience especially in religious matters"[30] In this section of my paper I will rely heavily on the thoughts of Pazhayampallil in his book 'Pastoral Guide' since I consider his work as very insightful. In his work he has enumerated the rights that full religious freedom implies[31] and I will name a few of them here: a) Freedom to hold or not to hold a particular faith; b) freedom to perform acts of prayer and worship, individually and collectively; c) freedom for families to choose the schools or other means which provide this sort of education for their children, without having to sustain directly or indirectly extra charges which would in fact deny them this freedom; d) freedom at personal, civic or social levels, from any form of coercion to perform acts contrary to one's faith, or to receive an education or to join groups or associations with principles opposed to one's religious convictions; e) freedom not to be subjected, on religious grounds, to forms of restriction and discrimination, vis-à-vis one's fellow citizens, in all aspects of life (career, study, employment and participation in civic or social responsibility).

Furthermore Thomas Pazhayampallil discussed the areas covered by religious freedom at the community and international level which counts among others: a) freedom for the various religious denominations, uniting believers of a given faith, to exist and act as social bodies organized according to their own doctrinal principles and institutional purposes; b) freedom to receive and publish religious books related to faith and worship, and to have free use of them; c)

---

[30] *Pastoral Guide Vol. 1, P.386*

[31] *Ibid. PP. 392-394*

freedom to proclaim and communicate the teaching of the faith, whether by the spoken or the written word, inside as well as outside places of worship, and to make known their moral teaching on human activities and on the organization of society; d) freedom, with regard to religious communities which, like the Catholic Church, to have a supreme authority responsible at the world level (in line with the directives of their faith) for the unity of communion that binds together all pastors and believers in the same confession.

His list is very extensive, but I have mentioned these few points just to highlight how all embracive the idea of religious freedom is. It is very central to the human person and that is why care must be taken to ensure that it is not trampled upon by any government authorities. In the words of the Second Vatican Council of the Catholic Church, "It is through his conscience that man sees and recognizes the demands of the divine law. He is bound to follow this conscience faithfully in all his activity so that he may come to God, who is his last end. Therefore he must not be forced to act contrary to his conscience. Nor must he be prevented from acting according to his conscience, especially in religious matters"[32] It is in recognition of the centrality of this right of the human person to aspire freely towards his creator that the right of freedom of religion has been guaranteed by the First Amendment to the US Constitution, the UN General Assembly and ratified by most countries in the world.

But we do know that there are still a lot of places in the world especially in Africa, Asia and Eastern Europe where religious liberty is either not fully practiced or even non-existent. In an article on 'Juicy Ecumenism' Nathaniel Torrey made the following observation, "To say the least, religious liberty's existence in that part of the world is precarious and sometimes practically non-existent. One of

---

[32] *Vatican Council II, Dignitatis Humanae #3*

the speakers had an entirely different person read his contribution so that he would not be punished by the law. This is in Uzbekistan, where practicing Christianity as effectively become "illegal, as any items connected to God, like calendars, posters, CDs, books, etc.- all become illegal to possess. Also any meeting of Christians, including parties and birthday celebrations, come under the category of unlawful religious activity!"[33] While in the western world the fight for religious liberty hovers around issues such as whether religious institutes should be mandated to provide insurance coverage for contraceptives or not and legalization of same sex marriage, places like Uzbekistan are dealing with the freedom for Christians to openly practice their faith without fear of punishment. Evidently there is still a lot of work to be done to ensure that the freedom of religion is upheld everywhere in the world.

Yet like other freedoms there are legitimate limits to freedom of religion. But let us be clear here, when we speak about limits of freedom of religion, the understanding is that what is controlled is the exercise and not the right itself. Thomas Pazhayampallil drew attention to J. Courtney Murray's footnotes on the Vatican II document, 'Dignitatis Humanae' where he wrote, "The right itself is always inalienable, never to be denied; only the exercise of the right is subject to control in particular instances"[34] Without getting into all the challenges in the courts with regard to what rights are guaranteed or not guaranteed under the freedom of religion act especially in the US, it is safe to say that in the exercise of their rights, individuals and religious groups must take care not to trample on the rights of other members of the community and to avoid public disorder. Freedom

---

[33] *The Institute on Religion & Democracy, Juicy Ecumenism (Feb 14, 2013) retrieved on July 20, 2015*

[34] *Pastoral Guide Vol. 1, P.391*

of religion does not give one the right to disregard justice and peace in society. As Pazhayampallil concluded, "The exercise of religious freedom, then, can be restricted by coercive force only when there is proof that it causes some violation of the rights of others or public peace or public morality"[35] Of course it has to be clearly established that there have been these violations according to the legitimate ordinances of the law of the Land.

Responding to the decision of the Supreme Court in Canada on February 27, 2013 in a landmark case regarding the distribution of anti-gay fliers by an individual in the name of freedom of religion, the Moderator of The United Church of Canada, the Right Rev. Gary Paterson, agreed that "Freedom of religion is not absolute. It does not include the right to engage in religiously motivated hate speech, and it does not extend to conduct that harms or interferes with the rights of others." Freedom of religion should not be used as a platform to promote bigotry, discrimination and spread hate speech. If there is something that it should do, it is to recognize diversity of beliefs and practices, and the freedom of every individual to live according to his/her conscience without interference from any person, authority or government.

d. Freedom to Petition the Government:

In the First Amendment the right/freedom to petition the government is often referred to as the *'Petition Clause'*. It states that "People have the right to appeal to government in favor of or against policies that affect them or in which they feel strongly. This freedom includes the right to gather signatures in support of a cause and

---

[35] *Ibid. P.392*

to lobby legislative bodies for or against legislation."[36] The usual understanding in the provisions of this right is that no individual or group maybe subjected to any punishment or harassment as a result of their effort to present requests to the government on their behalf or on behalf of another who feel concerned about any particular issue. The freedom to petition the government was always an important principle valued by the Founding Fathers because of their experience of trying to get King George III and Parliament to redress their grievances. In 1775, members of the Second Continental Congress had drafted a letter to the King seeking redress for what they considered harsh treatment from Britain. The grievances included such things as the king not obeying his own laws, preventing the people from establishing their own elected rulers, keeping standing armies in their land without their consent, imposing taxes without their consent, denying the right to trial by jury in some cases, encouraging the slave population to rebel against them and many others.[37] This petition has come to be known in history as the *Olive Branch Petition*. They had written the petition as their way of seeking a means to avoid a war of independence with Britain. But their petition was summarily turned down. In a speech to Parliament on 26 October 1775, King George III declared: "It has now become the part of wisdom, and (in its effects) of clemency, to put a speedy end to these disorders by the most decisive exertions."[38] The ensuing repercussion of this refusal was the American War of Independence.

It was to forestall that reoccurrence of such bitter and disappointing experience of the Founding Fathers that the provision was made in the

---

[36] *Elisia Hahnenberg (Learning to give.org), citing from 'The First Amendment Center' web site*

[37] *Revolutionary-war-and-beyond.com/freedom-of-petition-clause*

[38] *GoPetition – A leading global petition hosting service*

First Amendment for the right to Petition the government to become a fundamental right for every citizen. The role of James Madison, who was to later become the fourth President of the United States, in drafting the Petition Clause in the First Amendment has been hailed in history as monumental. The right to petition specifically prohibits Congress from abridging "the right of the people ... to petition the Government for redress of grievances."[39] This right presupposes that the individual has a right to complain and expects to be listened to by the relevant authorities. No one wants to feel they are not being listened to especially by a government that has been elected by the people for the people. However, as we have observed in reference to all other freedoms, petition to government must be done in a nonviolent way following all legal procedures. Petitions could be sent to any branch of government i.e. Executive, Legislative or Judiciary, and at any level including federal, state or local authorities. The right to petition any branch of government does not include the right to physically meet the official to whom the petition is addressed.

In as much as one would expect every right thinking government of the people to be open to receiving complains from the people about matters which concern them or their fellow citizens, the government is not required by the 'Petition Clause' to respond to every petition. This is what the position is, but in truth there have been so many challenges to this understanding with people insisting that there was no point in having the right to petition if the government was not required to respond. But in the case of the 'Magna Carta' of the United Kingdom which is close to the Freedom of Petition in the United States, a response by the relevant authorities to which the petition has been sent was always implied. An article written in the *'Revolutionary War and Beyond'* the author explains how the process

---

[39] *Ibid.*

of seeking redress had to work: "… if we, (referring to the King) or our justiciar, or our bailiffs or any one of our officers, shall in anything be at fault towards anyone, or shall have broken any one of the articles of this peace or of this security, and the offense be notified to four barons of the foresaid five and twenty, the said four barons shall repair to us (or our justiciar, if we are out of the realm) and, laying the transgression before us, petition to have that transgression redressed without delay. And if we shall not have corrected the transgression (or, in the event of our being out of the realm, if our justiciar shall not have corrected it) within forty days, reckoning from the time it has been intimated to us (or to our justiciar, if we should be out of the realm), the four barons aforesaid shall refer that matter to the rest of the five and twenty barons, and those five and twenty barons shall, together with the community of the whole realm, distrain and distress us in all possible ways, namely, by seizing our castles, lands, possessions, and in any other way they can, until redress has been obtained as they deem fit, saving harmless our own person, and the persons of our queen and children; and when redress has been obtained, they shall resume their old relations towards us."[40]

Without prejudice to the points already made about the importance of the Freedom of Petition, it must be observed that the Freedom to Petition may be restricted by the government with reasonable restrictions as to time, place and manner. Furthermore "Someone petitioning the government for redress of grievances must prove that they have legal standing in the matter, meaning that they must show that they are personally affected in the matter addressed"[41]. However it is considered unconstitutional for any government to use any means, either by force or the court of law to make it impossible for

---

[40] *Revolutionary-war-and-beyond.com/freedom-of-petition-clause*
[41] *Ibid*

any person or group from availing themselves of the right to petition. The various forms of the use of the right to Petition includes, but does not exhaust, "Lobbying, letter-writing, e-mail campaigns, testifying before tribunals, filing lawsuits, supporting referenda, collecting signatures for ballot initiatives, peaceful protests and picketing"[42]. In general the right to petition has worked better when people work together under a group because several voices are always louder than one. And this is where one has to acknowledge the great contributions of non- governmental organizations (NGO). These organizations which are also known as not for profit organizations, have been at the forefront of galvanizing citizens together to articulate better and channel their concerns to the relevant authorities. Among this group we can identify a few including: The American Civil Liberties Union (ACLU), Environmental Defense Network (EDN) and The Gay and Lesbian Alliance Against Defamation (GLAAD). The chances of succeeding with these groups are better than when an individual tries to go it alone.

Over the years, the Supreme Court of the United States has proved itself a strong organ of ensuring that the people's right to petition the government has been preserved and honored. There are several instances where the use of the Petition Clause has yielded positive results, but one that stands out would be the protest against segregation in the United States of America which was led by the Civil Rights movement. And we must be quick to underline the immense contribution of the Supreme Court in the success of this movement, as has been observed elsewhere, "During the civil rights movement, for example, the Supreme Court upheld the rights of several groups of individuals protesting segregation at public institutions such as

---

[42] *Elisia Hahnenberg (Learning to give.org), citing from 'The First Amendment Center' web site*

libraries and schools, and ruled that these citizens had every right to express their rights under the petition clause"[43]. The freedom of Petition is one of the fruits of a viable democracy; it is an uncommon reality in autocratic monarchies and mostly absent in totalitarian governments.

e. Freedom of the Press

Freedom of the Press has been described as "The right, guaranteed by the First Amendment to the U.S. Constitution, to gather, publish, and distribute information and ideas without government restriction; this right encompasses freedom from prior restraints on publication and freedom from Censorship"[44]. Dictionary.com defines it as the "The right to circulate opinions in print without censorship by the government". There have been discussions among scholars as to whether there was any significant difference between Freedom of the Press and Freedom of Speech. To buttress this point of the lack of substantial difference between the two freedoms, Chief Justice of the U.S. Supreme Court Warren E. Burger (1978) wrote in a landmark judgment delivered in the case of First National Bank of Boston v. Bellotti "Because the First Amendment was meant to guarantee freedom to express and communicate ideas, I can see no difference between the right of those who seek to disseminate ideas by way of a newspaper and those who give lectures or speeches and seek to enlarge the audience by publication and wide dissemination"[45]. Broadly the two freedoms seem to have the same objective and address the same concerns, yet there are technical distinctions that

---

[43] *Ibid.*

[44] *legal-dictionary.thefreedictionary.com – Freedom of the Press*

[45] *Ibid.*

warrant our treatment of the Freedom of the Press separately from the freedom of Speech in this inquiry.

It is understood that the press exercises enormous power and influence on the issues of the day and on governments, and even helps to form opinion of the masses about various issues. Journalists generally are in a more privileged position to have easier and better access to information than the rest of the people, and as such are often referred to as the eyes, the ears and voices of the people. They can prop up a government as well as tear it down by what they say and write. Their responsibility is significant and therefore talk about their freedom in their line of duty should be treated slightly different from the usual freedom of speech discussion. There is a non-profit group known as the '*Freedom House*' which has dedicated itself to the service of monitoring freedom of the press around the world since 1980. In an article on its homepage, the group underlined the need for a free press when it observed that "a free press plays a key role in sustaining and monitoring a healthy democracy, as well as in contributing to greater accountability, good government, and economic development. Most importantly, restrictions on media are often an early indicator that governments intend to assault other democratic institutions". This goes a long way to confirm the general understanding of the media as the watchdog for the people.

The freedom of the press as envisaged in the First Amendment includes the freedom from prior restraints. This simply means the restraint on a publication before it is published. The long held conviction of legal scholars is that prior restraints are presumptively unconstitutional. As Reporters Committee for Freedom of the Press, a nonprofit association dedicated to assisting journalists since 1970, remarked, "This is so because they carry a heavy burden to sustain and are rarely upheld. In its 1931 landmark opinion, Nebraska Press

Association v. Stuart, the U.S. Supreme Court described prior restraints on speech and publication as "the most serious and the least tolerable infringement on First Amendment rights." However the Court identified three types of publications against which a prior restraint might be valid: those that pose a threat to national security, those that advocate violence or the overthrow of the government and those that contain obscene materials. It is important to point out that the objection to the use of the doctrine of prior restraint in the issue of obscene materials may be based upon the proposition that obscenity is not a protected form of expression. Here, I think, it is a proper position to take. Even if one were to be punished after the publication of obscene materials, the harm done to society by the fact of the publication is an irreparable one. It is under such consideration that I think the relevant authorities would be right to restrain such publications. Yet care must be taken to ensure that the right process is observed to avoid abuse of power. As has been observed several times in court cases involving the 'Prior Restraint' clause, "the thrust of the Court's opinions in this area with regard to all forms of communication has been to establish strict standards of procedural protections to ensure that the censoring agency bears the burden of proof on obscenity, that only a judicial order can restrain exhibition, and that a prompt final judicial decision is assured".[46]

A further term that merits our particular attention in the freedom of the press is censorship. According to the *Free Dictionary*, censorship is "the suppression or proscription of speech or writing that is deemed obscene, indecent, or unduly controversial". In general it is a means that most autocratic governments in the world adopt to keep the press in check and destroy any opposition to their policies. It is always considered a bad idea and especially in the USA and other

---

[46] *See more at: http://constitution.findlaw.com/amendment1/annotation09*

democracies in the world, it is unconstitutional. It is an infringement on the freedom of the press and by extension an infringement on human rights. It is in the light of this that the First Amendment to the US Constitution abhors the term censorship in general in the provision on the right of the citizens to freedom of the press.

Yet there are areas in which both the courts and even common sense indicate that there could be censorship in order to protect the public. Such areas include books used in schools, Prisoners' mail, the internet, music, art and the entertainment industry. Censorship is necessary as it relates to books used in schools for the fact that there have been times when parents have pointed out that certain books contain objectionable ideas springing from either political, moral or religious grounds. When such instances occur, school boards or school districts have always responded by banning such books entirely or removing them from the schools' libraries. I believe that students have a right to be protected from harmful materials and the onus is on the parents and school authorities to act accordingly to ensure the protection of the students. Granted some people may argue that the right of free expression is being truncated by this act, but they should bear in mind that as a society we owe it as a duty to the future generation to hand on to them some decent values. Another area that I am convinced censorship would be proper is the idea of control of information in and out of the prison. This is very necessary in order to ensure that there are no plans hatched by prisoners or their associates to bring about their escape from prison. It is in the interest of the general public that a check is kept on the communication between prisoners and the outside world. Unfortunately the prisoners lost their freedom when they abused it in the first place by making the wrong choices.

Just like other freedoms, freedom of the press does not grant an absolute right to the press. For the purposes of national security and in times of war, the press is expected to act with responsibility in order not to give away information that might jeopardize the security of the soldiers and the public. Furthermore freedom of the press does not protect the right to publish scurrilous, defamatory, and libelous materials. The general 'harm principle' still holds with regard to the freedom of the press for the courts in the land have always held that journalists were not invested with special privileges that could allow them to publish whatever they want irrespective of the fact that it may harm the good name of another. To check the excesses of the press, there is in place what is generally known as defamation law. This has been the way most states in the United States have dealt with false statements, slander and libel (including criminal libel). The defamation law has granted a lot of security and reprieve to businesses and public figures, who without this protection would have been left at the mercy of the press, especially the print media.

III. Limits to our freedom

In as much as we recognize that freedom is a natural right to every individual, there are still boundaries that are set for the protection of the individual and also for society as a whole. For instance free as a parent may like the child to be, it is always understood that there have to be restraints in order to protect the child from wandering into harmful situations or picking up dangerous objects. In the same light even adults could be restrained from engaging in acts which could be judged as certainly dangerous and would ultimately lead to death. One should not be free to get drunk and endanger the lives of others. It is to be borne in mind at all times that one's freedom to extend one's arms should stop at the point that the arms reaches another person's face. In short as John Stuart Mill observed, "The liberty of the individual must be thus far limited; he must not make himself a nuisance to other people"[47] Thomas Jefferson also agreed with this position when he said, "Of liberty I would say that, in the whole plenitude of its extent, it is unobstructed action according to our will. But rightful liberty is unobstructed action according to our will within limits drawn around us by the equal rights of others. I do not add 'within the limits of the law,' because law is often but the tyrant's will, and always so when it violates the right of an individual." --Thomas Jefferson to I. Tiffany, 1819.[48]

These boundaries often are natural and seek to protect the physical and moral good of the individual in question, yet they could be imposed by just laws which seek to preserve law and order in society. It is to this angle of restriction of one's freedom that John Stuart Mill spoke in his book on Liberty where he wrote, "The only purpose for which power can be rightfully exercised over any member of a civilized community against his will, is to prevent harm to others"[49] Continuing he said, "Whenever, in short, there is a definite damage, or a definite risk of damage, either to an individual or to the public, the case is taken out of the province of liberty and placed in that of morality or law".[50] Without prejudice to his stated opinion above with regard to the law, Thomas Jefferson had earlier commented on the role of law in checking the dangerous exercise of freedom in his 'Official Opinion' in 1790 that "All natural rights may be abridged or modified in their exercise by law." --Thomas Jefferson: Official

---

[47] *Today's Moral Issues, P.152*

[48] *The Jeffersonian Perspective: Commentary on Today's Social and Political Issues Based on the Writings of Thomas Jefferson.*

[49] *Today's Moral Issues, P. 146*

[50] *Ibid. P. 154*

Opinion, 1790.[51] Jefferson like so many other right thinking people in life saw government and freedom as two sides of the same coin, and believed that there should always be limitations and restraints both to excessive, oppressive governments and the individual's exercise of one's natural rights to freedom.

On his part Edmund Burke argued that the individual's liberty is as important as public harmony, order and justice; consequently there are certain group of persons who should be rightly deprived of their freedom because of the menace they constitute to civilized society. Rhetorically he asked, "Is it because liberty in the abstract may be classed amongst the blessings of mankind that I am seriously to felicitate a madman, who has escaped from the protecting restraint and wholesome darkness of his cell, on his restoration to enjoyment of light and liberty? Am I to congratulate a highwayman and murderer who has broken prison upon recovery of his natural rights?"[52] In other words, by their behavior or disposition, certain persons unfortunately limit their own freedom, and give society grounds to suspend their entitlement to liberty. The circumstances surrounding their cases suggest that their freedom be suspended or limited. Put differently, these kind of individuals have willingly or unwillingly relinquished their rights to freedom and the onus is on the state to ensure that they pay the full price for their behavior.

Elsewhere Burke would insist that "Liberty without wisdom and virtue is the greatest of all evils; for it is folly, vice, and madness, without tuition and restraint."[53] Continuing he said, "As to the right

---

[51] *The Jeffersonian Perspective: Commentary on Today's Social and Political Issues Based on the Writings of Thomas Jefferson.*

[52] *Today's Moral Issues, P. 141*

[53] *Edmund Burke: Champion of Ordered Liberty by John Attarian, an article in The Intercollegiate Review—Fall 1997*

of men to act anywhere according to their pleasure, without any moral tie, no such right exists. Men are never in a state of total independence of each other."[54] There cannot be such thing as an absolute right to freedom especially when we recognize that man is a social being and whatever an individual does has an effect not only on the acting agent, but also on those other persons who are in relationship with him. Truth is, even if we believed that we are so free that we can do anything we want, the reality is that the freedom of other people will definitely have to put a check on our freedom. This is both an existential and moral imperative, as well as a reality as a result of the cultural and political exigencies of our world. In the next chapter I shall examine the concept of freedom from the existentialist point of view.

---

[54] *Ibid.*

CHAPTER 2

FREEDOM AND EXISTENTIALISM

I. The Existentialist thinking

In the previous chapter, I have largely discussed what could easily pass as political/civil concept of freedom in which I stated that freedom and liberty could be used interchangeably. I also elaborated on the implications of the freedom of speech, assembly and religion, and of course insisted that there were recognizable and legitimate limits to human freedoms. In the present chapter I will examine freedom from the existentialist point of view. In existentialism, freedom is always linked to responsibility; to seek freedom without assuming the responsibility entailed is unhealthy in the mind of the existentialist. And for the records, I agree with this position. Existentialism does not allow one to use the feeling of powerlessness to excuse one from exercising one's freedom. Even though the many factors that go into making us and our experience are determined, we can arrange them as we like. We are free to make of them, and ourselves, whatever we will. I will like to use the case of Viktor Frankl to bring out the existentialist thinking as it concerns freedom and meaning in life.

II. The man Viktor Frankl

Viktor Frankl was born in Vienna, Austria on March 26, 1905 and died on September 2, 1997. By the age of 25years he already had acquired a doctor of medicine and went on to acquire a PhD in 1949. He was a professor of Neurology and Psychiatry at the University of Vienna Medical School. He got married to his first wife, Tilly Grosser in 1941, who died in 1945. Between 1940 and 1942 Frankl was director of the Neurological Department of the Rothschild Hospital. In the year 1942 Viktor's life took a dramatic turn, for it was then that he, together with his wife, parents and brother were arrested in Vienna. He would go on to spend a full 3years of his life in various concentration camps during World War II. Auschwitz especially would come to stand out for him for it was during his transfer to this particular camp that he lost a manuscript that was so dear to him. And he was to agonize over this loss for most of his time in the concentration camp. Viktor and his fellow prisoners suffered terribly in the hands of their German captors. Yes they were physically tortured, but the psychological and mental torture he went through became for Dr. Viktor Frankl a whole new lesson on the being called man. He would then go on to publish a master piece of a book "Man's Search for Meaning" in 1946 after his release from the concentration camp. In this book he has outlined his psychotherapeutic method of counseling known as logotherapy. I will proceed to discuss some of the themes expounded by Dr. Viktor Frankl.

The case of Viktor Frankl, the Austrian psychiatrist and Holocaust survivor, stands as a validation of the position that we are free to choose what to make of our situation and how to respond to the events that occur in our lives when he described his experience in the concentration camp in his book, *Man's Search for Meaning.* At a point he asked the questions, "Is there no spiritual freedom in regard to behavior and reaction to any given surroundings? Does man not have a choice of action in the face of such circumstances"? He was to provide an answer to his questions based on his own experience and what he saw from other inmates in the camp, "Man can preserve a vestige of spiritual freedom, of independence of mind, even in such terrible conditions of psychic and physical stress"[55] In his conclusion, he asserted that "It is this spiritual freedom –which cannot be taken away – that makes life meaningful and purposeful"[56]

Viktor Frankl counsels that freedom is only to be regarded as authentic when it is coupled with responsibleness. As he observed, "in fact, freedom is in danger of degenerating into mere arbitrariness unless it is lived in terms of responsibleness"[57] This freedom that is aligned with responsibleness is very reasonable and allows itself to go through a very careful thought process. It asks the relevant questions such as: what ought a man created in the image and likeness of God do in a given situation? How does my choice enhance my nature as a member of the community of individuals? Does this particular action destroy or ultimately ensure my happiness? Of course it asks the question, is pleasure invariably equal to happiness? This is a position that has been collaborated by an existential psychotherapist Leslie Spivak, when he wrote, "Freedom cannot be taught directly because it signifies the unique individual struggle of the person to attain and maintain adulthood; and since freedom can only be self-defined, it

---

[55] *Man's Search for Meaning, P.86*

[56] *Ibid. P.87*

[57] *Ibid. P. 156*

is up to each individual to find it for himself."[58] In order to act freely, however, one must not let one's action be determined by just any of one's particular desires or interests. The individual must act as any free agent would act, hence one must act as one would like other people to act.

The reality called man is very complex in the sense that he could at one time be attributed with the noblest of characters and yet at another time could sink to the depths of depravity in his actions. Man is both gifted with the capacity to be free and burdened with certain conditions arising from his environment. The truly integrated and free individual has to constantly make decisions about himself and the world around him. The question is: How would he choose? This is the question that Viktor Frankl has carefully addressed in the concept of Collective neurosis and made his final submission when he wrote, "Man has potentialities within himself; which one is actualized depends on decisions but not on conditions"[59] No one is allowed to hide under the excuse that their conditions could not allow them to do otherwise neither should one let oneself just flow with the current no matter where it goes. The individual with character would have to swim against the current most often in life. In Frankl's view, when we speak about freedom, "It is not freedom from conditions, but it is freedom to take a stand toward the conditions"[60] Freedom is not something we find outside the walls of a prison; in fact an individual could be in prison and still experience freedom because he is able to envision a future and makes every effort to realize this

---

[58] *An Application of Kierkegaard's Philosophy of Freedom to Psychotherapy and Philosophical Counseling*

[59] *Man's Search for Meaning, P. 157*

[60] *Ibid. P.153*

future. Freedom is about how an individual chooses to respond to a particular situation at a given time.

Granted, the search for meaning was paramount for Viktor, Dr. Morgan, as well as other commentators, agrees that he was not just seeking meaning within himself and for himself alone. He was using his perceived freedom to ask the important questions. And it is this attitude that sets Viktor's theory apart from Freud (will to pleasure) and Adler (will to power). Viktor somehow knew that he had to go beyond himself in order to find meaning. Dr. Morgan has been very helpful in exposing us to sources that seem to understand Viktor well enough to lead us into his deepest thoughts. The intervention of the Jewish Rabbi, Heschel, comes handy here to lead us into the area of the 'transcendent thou' which Viktor contemplated, even if he did not speak of it as directly as one would expect a Jewish scholar: "Tell man he is an end within himself and his answer will be despair"[61] In other words to live a life conscious of God is an endless hope, while a life without God is a hopeless end. Our life, hope and meaning come from God; to turn away from God produces all kinds of evil and subsequently meaninglessness and ultimately extinction without significance. Victor might not have had the typical religious man's view of God, however, he knew that it was important to hold on to this idea of a 'transcendent thou' without whom life and meaning were impossible. In this he shows that he identifies with the aspiration of every human person who is consciously or unconsciously clinging to something or rather someone (even if it is just a hope that someone might be waiting for one at the other end) beyond oneself in order to find freedom and ultimately, meaning in life. His theory is not from out of space, it is credible and as Dr. Morgan said, it is

---

[61] *John Morgan, Naturally Good*

"quite defensible both in terms of existential psychology and Jewish philosophy"[62]

The whole focal point of Viktor Frankl's psychotherapy was on the will to meaning which was a theory that, unlike psychoanalysis and other related disciplines which delved into the past of the individual, offered hope and promise to the individual in a future that one can live for. The future meant so much to Viktor and his fellow prisoners, as he observed at a point, "The prisoner who had lost faith in the future – his future – was doomed"[63] Logotherapy is indeed a positive science that is investing on looking at the best in the individual instead of spending enormous energy trying to dig up the worst in a person. Its starting point is the presumption that in every individual there is the good that if well harnessed can produce the best. It is in the fulfillment of one's potentials that one finds the meaning for one's life. The search for and pursuit of this fulfillment is so very important and can so consume an individual that as Viktor observed, "Man, however is able to live and die for the sake of his ideals and values"[64]

A failure to identify and embark on the journey of fulfilling one's potentials, leaves one's existence devoid of meaning and consequently empty and sad, whether one is conscious of the situation or not. And there have been people who have been left sad and empty without really knowing what has been going on in their lives. These kinds of individuals have nothing to live for and know of nothing or anybody they could die for. As we say in every day parlance, you either stand for something or be prepared to fall for anything. Life for this group of individuals would just be floating with the current and they can

---

[62] *Ibid. P. 151*

[63] *Viktor E. Frankl, Man's Search for Meaning, P. 95*

[64] *Ibid. P. 121*

never attempt to swim against the current. The good news however, is that a large proportion of human beings are interested and desirous of finding out the meaning of their lives. Obviously, Viktor Frankl in his theory of the will to meaning is on to something that's real and needed today.

Getting involved with Logotherapy which emphasizes the theory of will to meaning does not make one a mental patient (there is nothing wrong with the individual); one is simply an enquirer, a regular human person trying to understand where he is and where he could possibly go. This individual is faced with a situation of concern and as Viktor Frankl clarified, "A man's concern, even his despair, over the worthwhileness of life is an existential distress but by no means a mental disease"[65] Rather the one that has a problem is the individual who is content with just sitting there and going where ever the wind blows, without asking any questions. One of the early Greek philosophers had said that 'an unexamined life is not worth living', this could be applied here in a positive sense. As it concerns the case of the theory of will to meaning, it is not an examination to find fault in my past rather an examination aimed at assessing what meaning my life has and as to how I can best fulfill the meaning of my life. It is not about resolving a conflict of personality; it is about fulfilling the best me. In this is my freedom.

This search for meaning may awaken some 'monsters' in the individual, I mean disturb the 'peace' that one thought he had and there are persons who could quit from the search for the meaning of their lives just because of this upsetting of their system. In this case some might begin to wonder if it was necessary to disorganize peoples' lives or disconcert them with this process. But Viktor Frankl rightly countered, "I consider it a dangerous misconception of mental

---

[65] *Ibid. P.125*

hygiene to assume that what man needs in the first place is equilibrium or, as it is called in biology, 'homeostasis', i.e. a tensionless state"[66] For Viktor, tension is a necessary tool in the process of one realizing the meaning of one's life, otherwise one is like a contented sow, just ok with life and there is nothing to aspire towards and maybe nothing to hope for. What a life that would be.

It is very important that one realizes that one has not arrived yet; there must always be this anticipation in one's life to make life exciting and worth living. The constant strive for growth is natural to the human person and it is the one sure way that one can realize the meaning of one's life. One has to live with this awareness that one's life is not empty of meaning, and it is this awareness that will motivate him to embark on the process that ultimately will bring him to the meaning of his life. To stop the search is synonymous with giving up on life and all the hopes and promises that life holds for us. In spite of Viktor Frankl's situation in the concentration camp, he still had that awareness or maybe the hope that his life and that of his fellow prisoners meant something more than the brutality that they received from the guards. For them the meaning of their lives was not dependent on what they received from the world, but what the world expected from them. As Viktor puts it, "it did not really matter what we expected from life, but rather what life expected from us"[67] And somewhere, even if it was in their unconscious self, they knew they had to deliver. And this is how we should approach life, seeking to fulfill ourselves in realizing that which we owe to life. We cannot just be passive observers in life; we have to be active participants. And this is why suicide is not the answer; it is simply cowardice, an escape

---

[66] *Ibid. P. 127*

[67] *Ibid. P. 98*

from responsibility and calling it quits with so much on the line not just for us, but for the rest of humanity.

III.   What is Freedom in Existentialism?

According to existentialism freedom is identical with existence. "Freedom is the totality of human existence in one's environment, involving both choices and responsibilities, for man is always free within his situation to choose the meaning in his life, free to reconstruct his interpretation of experience, free to reassess and alter them if he chooses"[68] For existentialists freedom essentially means existence which in transcending the mold of norms cast round it, reaches to and finds the real potentialities of its being. The individual embarks on a process through what Nietzsche terms the 'autonomous conscience' in which he is able to emancipate himself from all the constraints that otherwise tamed him. At the end of this process, in Nietzsche's thinking "stands the radically sovereign individual – the individual who, in this moment of 'proud knowledge' that he has won freedom and power 'over himself and over fate', first gains for himself his own personal responsibility"[69]

In speaking about existentialism and freedom, my mind goes right away to the massive contribution of the Christian existentialist, Soren Kierkegaard (1813-1855), who insisted that human freedom has its origin from God, and humanity can only truly be free by allowing God to be the absolute in the world. He acknowledged that in the human person there is an unlimited desire and aspiration that could cause him anxiety and a sense of uncertainty. As Golam

---

[68] *The Interpreted World: An Introduction to Phenomenological Psychology by Ernesto Spinelli, P.116 (1989)*

[69] *Johannes B. Metz, Moral Evil Under Challenge, P.73*

Dastagir expressed it in his article *'Existentialist Concept of Freedom and Morality'*, according to Kierkegaard, "there is in human being no responsibility which can be said limited and specific, for man desires to outdo himself and to be other than what he himself is"[70]. Golam summarized that for Kierkegaard "the exact meaning of freedom is commitment to action which helps man to build up himself as a man of full sense of liability". Man feels the weight of responsibility and wants to commit himself to some actions, to assert himself as a free human person, able to act and become more. Still man is afraid of what he can think of and do with his freedom. For Kierkegaard, the solution to this situation is the individual's attachment to God for direction and meaning. However his position that freedom has already been determined by God has made his critics to wonder if actually there is anything like true freedom for the individual if everything is done at God's command. And if everything has been predetermined for man and is done according to God's command, then man cannot be held responsible for his actions.

Some scholars have made attempts to reconcile the issue of determinism and freewill. One example that comes to mind would be that of John Warwick Montgomery who wrote, "In spite of Herculean efforts to arrive at rational compatibility between genetic determinism and freely chosen human actions, the paradox remains: in theory, our acts are predetermined, yet in practice we must take personal responsibility for them in order to maintain a functioning civilized society. Einstein put it succinctly: "I am a determinist, compelled to act as if free will existed, because if I wish to live in a civilized society, I must act responsibly. I know philosophically a murderer is not responsible for his crimes, but I prefer not to take tea

---

[70] *Published in Jibon Darshan – a Research Journal of Philosophy, Jagannath University, Dhaka, Bangladesh, vol. 1, 2007*

with him.'"[71] Whatever be the case, the one thing that Kierkegaard and many other existentialist philosophers agree with is that every individual is free enough to make choices and that the individual must take responsibility for every choice of action he/she makes. There is no escaping from responsibility for any actions one takes – it belongs to the perpetrator and responsibility cannot be shifted to another, not even to genetic issues or societal failure.

IV. Concept of freedom in atheistic existentialism

Since after Kierkegaard a brand of existentialism has remained on the rise, an existentialism that is more humanistic or atheistic. This brand of existentialism boasts of illustrious philosophers such as Friedrich Nietzsche and Martin Heidegger, but has as its most prominent scholar, Jean Paul Sartre (1905-1980). In general this brand of existentialism, in relation to freedom proceeds from a notion developed by Immanuel Kant that freedom equals to autonomy. Freedom is not about some random or arbitrary choice making, rather it is a deliberate decision of an individual in recognition of one's responsibility to oneself and the world to commit oneself to certain principle/law. The common belief of this philosophical school runs thus: Human beings bear total responsibility for their choices. Human beings are responsible for how they exercise their freedom. Human beings determine their own morality and bear responsibility for how they do so. Human beings choose not just for themselves but for everyone else with each choice they make, they set examples and encourage others to act likewise. Human beings are radically free. So, humans are responsible for the consequences of

---

[71] *John Warwick Montgomery, The Freewill Issue in Theological Perspective published in Global Journal of Classic Theology, Vol. 8, no. 2*

their actions. Humans are responsible for what is happening to their world. There is no 'god' to set things right. If there is, that 'god' does not intervene into human freedom (affairs). Thus humans are totally responsible for all that they do and all that results from it[72]. This is a summary position of Jean Paul Sartre. In this chapter I will spend a fair amount of time and space discussing Sartre's concept of freedom which hinges principally on his understanding of existence and the individual's responsibility in the context of a non-existent God.

V.   Jean Paul Sartre

Jean-Paul Sartre was born in Paris in 1905. He was to be raised by his grandfather, Charles Schweitzer, from his mother's side having lost his father at a very early age. Interestingly Sartre was a great nephew of Albert Schweitzer. After all the turbulence of his early years through high school, Sartre eventually graduated from the prestigious Ecole Normale Superieure in 1929. During his many travels and studies, he studied in Berlin the writings of two great German philosophers, Edmund Husserl and Martin Heidegger, and this was to have an enormous influence in his development of what he would term atheistic existentialism. Sartre had lived his younger years during the tumult in Europe of the period of the First and Second World Wars, and he saw firsthand the brutality of men towards each other. He had become an activist especially through his writing hoping to help humanity discover the true meaning of existence. He is regarded today as a great phenomenological and existential philosopher and also a literary giant in Europe and around the world. He died in 1980, but his many works in literature and

---

[72] *An article on Freedom and Determinism by Phillip A. Pecorino sourced from the internet*

philosophy are eloquent testimonies of his contributions to the cause of human freedom and self-realization.

Going through Dr. John Morgan's overview of Jean Paul Sartre in his book, *Naturally Good*, one thing that struck me so powerfully was the 'consistently inconsistent' position of Sartre in a number of issues. For one who was passionate about man's freedom, I did not find him as affirming man enough, even as he made effort to enthrone man as the ultimate. For him, 'man is a useless passion', he is constantly on strife, and does not know peace. Could this be as a result of his experience during the World War II? As Sartre wrote in one of his works "*Situations*" and Dr. Morgan observed, "Man is not the sum of what he has but the totality of what he does not yet have, of what he might have"[73] He further implied in another work of his as Dr. Morgan highlighted, that "no one can really respect the freedom of others", yet in his other work, *'Existentialism and Humanism'*, he seemed to have taught that "the pursuit of one's own freedom requires one to promote the freedom of others, and that each individual is responsible to all for the values affirmed by each person's way of life"[74] A close following of his thought pattern would probably lead one to ask: so what did Sartre really believe and what did he want to communicate to his audience?

Sartre faithful to his existential principle that 'existence preceded essence', denied that there was anything like human nature, rather what mattered was what each individual was doing at any given time. Activity of an individual and not the idea of a human nature was what counted. This is only the necessary conclusion after it has been discovered that "God does not exist", Sartre insisted. Dr. Morgan accentuated the thoughts of Sartre well, when he wrote, "in a world

---

[73] *John H. Morgan, Naturally Good – P. 115.*

[74] *Ibid. P.115*

after God, humanity must learn to create for ourselves meaning and purpose".[75] Convinced that there is no God to look up to, humanity now realizes that the onus is on us to take care of ourselves, assume the role of creators and accept full responsibilities for our actions and inactions. We have to take the blame or the praise, whichever one is applicable, as a result of our choices. And this realization naturally causes the individual a bout of anxiety.

Unfortunately, as events that did unfold during Sartre's life time and those that continue to unfold this day show, humanity has not done a good job at taking responsibility for the world. While so many especially Christians look at these struggles and wished that humanity will recognize that we needed to return to God and entrust our being and our world to him, Sartre constantly pointed at them (including the World Wars and the attendant German occupation that he experienced) as an accomplishment of the human spirit. Dr. Morgan had highlighted the way Sartre framed the argument: Who is gloomier, "Is it the citizen on the street who systematically opts out of possible choice making situations because of some childishly assumed cosmic plan or divine scheme, or the existentialist who recognizes that whatever meaning and purpose there is in life, it is a creation of ourselves who choose to act"?[76] In Sartre's understanding, a bad choice was better than a no-choice.

In fact in one of his responses to the experience of the German occupation in an essay titled *"La Republique du Silence"* written in 1944 as highlighted by John Gerassi in his book on *Jean-Paul Sartre: hated conscience of his century,* Sartre said, "Never have we been as free as during the German occupation... Since the Nazi venom snuck even into our thoughts, every correct thought was a conquest; since

---

[75] *Ibid. P. 119*

[76] *John H. Morgan, Naturally Good, 121*

an all-powerful police tried to keep us silent, every word became precious like a declaration of principle; since we were watched, every gesture had the weight of a commitment... The very cruelty of the enemy pushed us to the extremity of the human condition by forcing us to ask the questions which we can ignore in peacetime"[77] This event was for Sartre a very defining moment in the understanding of the notion of freedom; what are people ready to do when faced with difficult situations? Would people just accept any situation without a fight (this is collaboration) or would they stand up to be counted (this is freedom)?

Sartre in line with the foundational principle of existentialism preached and promoted subjectivism as the only veritable option for humans. Man had to choose, take responsibility, and cannot make reference to anything or being beyond man. Any notion of the transcendence was nonsensical to him; a definite limit has been placed on the human person. With the rejection of the transcendent came the rejection of a universal human nature, however if there was any universal concept, it was a universal human condition. And what was this universal human condition? It was that of forlornness, anguish and despair (hopelessness). What a wretched condition? And yet Sartre claims that "Man is the future of man". Dr. Morgan has summarized this future that man has for his fellow according to Sartre and the atheistic existentialism, "condemned to life, free to act", in other words "we are condemned because we did not create ourselves, yet free because we are responsible for the way we conceive and will ourselves and all others to be"[78] Interestingly, given the thought pattern of Sartre, existence, freedom, consciousness and even nothingness are synonymous terms.

---

[77] *Gerassi John, Jean-Paul Sartre: hated conscience of his century.*

[78] *Ibid. P. 125*

VI. Subjectivism at the root of freedom

The core belief of atheistic existentialism is the absence of God, i.e. there is no principle or being beyond man. This existentialism "declares that every truth and every action implies a human setting and a human subjectivity"[79]. As it were, everything begins and ends with man. This is an unparalled enthronement of man. There is no question of anything happening to man out of chance, rather it is out of his choice or lack of choice, which in itself is a choice. There is nobody or being out there doing anything to man or for man; man is simply in charge of his life. Man is a product of his present activity, there is no past and no future plan, what counts is the 'now'. This is the meaning of freedom for Sartre; existence is equal to freedom. Sartre's concept of freedom simply put is autonomy of choice.

Existentialism as preached by Sartre claims that existence preceded essence. This assertion dismisses all we have known from the very start of philosophical and theological thinking that existence followed on essence. There had always been the understanding that there were already certain given in life which every human person was to make an effort to discover, and doing so was man's existence. But Sartre insists that "Man is nothing else but what he makes of himself."[80] By proposing that existence precedes essence, Sartre implies that man has no fixed nature and that we have not been made for any particular purpose. Of course there is no God to conceive a human nature. I suppose he is saying existence which he recognizes as accidental becomes the principle and then man has to decide what to make of one's self. Each individual now has the onerous task of making his or her own essence, and of course the obvious implication

---

[79] Jean Paul Sartre, *Existentialism and Human Emotions* – P. 10
[80] *Ibid. P. 15*

is that whatever we make of ourselves will equally be true for every human person. This gives man an unbounded and unlimited freedom to be whatever he/she wants. But the fear I have with this system is that it defies the logic of life; it says to me that a part is the sum total of the whole, instead of the whole being the sum total of the individual parts.

Sartre insisted that man is 'condemned to be free' and this means he is responsible for creating everything in the world, and everything assumes whatever meaning he gives it. As Sartre puts it, "he (*man*) is the one by whom it happens that there is a world; since he is also the one who makes himself be, then whatever may be the situation in which he finds himself... He must assume the situation with the proud consciousness of being the author of it..."[81] The individual is not just free and choosing from what is out there; rather he is freely creating what he wants to be out there. Yet there are scores of scholars who though acknowledge the freedom of man to his thoughts and actions, recognize that there are better ways in which a man can apply his power and intelligence. The well read English author, James Allen has made a very pertinent observation in his book *As A Man Thinketh* where he said, "As a being of power, intelligence and love, and the lord of his own thoughts, man holds the key to every situation, and contains within himself the transforming and regenerative agency by which he may make himself what he wills". However, he continued, "Man is always the master, even in his weakest and most abandoned state; but in his weakness and degradation he is the foolish master who misgoverns his 'household'"[82]. This is the sad reality of man left on his own.

Sartre considers freedom as the only ethical response of the

---

[81] *Jean Paul Sartre, Existentialism and Human Emotions – PP52-53*

[82] *James Allen, As A Man Thinketh, P.6*

individual who must at every point assume responsibility of the situation that one is faced with as his/her own. Sartre uses the example of a war (I presume he was speaking about the World War II which he lived through) to buttress the point when he wrote, "If therefore I have preferred war to death or to dishonor, everything takes place as if I bore the entire responsibility for this war"[83] In effect it doesn't really matter what I did or what I did not do, the fact is that I exist through the war, "therefore it remains for me only to lay claim to this war". Man is not left with options here, and that's what I believe Sartre means when he claimed that the individual has no excuse. But where then is the freedom for which we were made? Is it only the freedom to embrace the war or commit suicide? How do I convince myself that I am responsible for a war I know nothing about? So I also have to take responsibility for a vehicle hitting me as I sit in the front porch of my house? I mean how far can an individual go in taking responsibility for whatever happens around him/her? Obviously this is all as a result of the non-existence of God which the atheistic existentialist posited. And for me when and where God is not recognized, nothing looks right.

Sartre inevitably reduces one's existence to one's responsibility. My responsibility is who I am, as he writes, "Thus totally free, undistinguishable from the period for which I have chosen to be the meaning, as profoundly responsible for the war as if I had myself declared it, unable to live without integrating it in my situation..."[84] This inability to separate man from his responsibility or 'irresponsibility' gives the individual a limited definition, even as Sartre posits man as absolute and unlimited because of his perceived or presumed freedom. If this is all that man is worth, then we are

---

[83] *Ibid. PP54-55*

[84] *Ibid. p.56*

in a terrible shape; and I believe that is why Sartre summed up the condition of man in such dire words as anguish, forlornness and despair. Maybe it is this understanding of freedom that introduces the notion that so many have that 'it is not safe to be free'. Freedom that is determined by the individual alone, without considering factors outside of the individual, is always inadequate; so often it is interpreted to mean license to do what I want, when and how I want it, including taking one's life and the lives of others. After all who else matters in determining what I could do and could not do?

It is true that Sartre in speaking about freedom is not dealing specifically with the moral implications; however the Christian in me would not allow me to engage in any discussion on freedom without looking at it from the moral ambient. Servais Pinckaers, a priest of the Dominican order and a moral theologian underlined the importance of freedom to humans when he wrote: "Freedom is at the heart of our existence"[85] But we have to be wary of freedom of indifference which William Ockham taught and which I see as close to the existentialist idea where we are witnessing the enthronement of subjectivism. At the center of every decision and action was the individual's self-interest. Obviously it was this kind of concept of freedom that Thomas Hobbes was so worried about that he warned in his book, *Leviathan*, that if individuals within a society continually lived by their own self-interests, they would continue to hurt each other and be stuck in a "state of war." Freedom of indifference, akin to atheistic existentialism, craved autonomy for humanity and did away with any form of dependence, even dependence on God. This is a recipe for chaos in society, for each individual could make his own law according to his own choosing at any given instance. How can we ensure that the freedoms of others are respected without trampling

---

[85] *Pinckaers Servais, OP- The Sources of Christian Ethics P.238*

on the freedom of this one individual? Interestingly even Marxism would later condemn this individualism as running contrary to the solidarity among human beings that Marxism was promoting. It would consider this idea of each individual being able to choose and become what they wished as a luxury that can only be afforded by the bourgeoisie. At the end of the day it becomes obvious that only God and the moral law should be the guarantor of our freedom.

VII.   The Hole

Jean Paul Sartre described the hole "as a nothingness 'to be filled' with my own flesh"[86]. Each time man sees an empty space, he is inclined to find a way to fill it with something, even if it is his own being. I have seen this severally in little 2 year olds trying to crawl into empty cupboards in kitchens, under the bed, etc. Growing up too I saw situations where as kids we tried to block our nostrils with little pebbles, stones, etc. As Sartre explained, so many children are found with their fingers in their mouth, noses and indeed any opening in their bodies. Children are constantly plugging holes. But these are not just physical appearances; Sartre sees in them a deeper existential and psychological implication. And I do agree with him. This is man's way of seeking to be the absolute, to create and to be in control.

The foregoing is consistent with the desire in man to be God. This desire which is like an unquenchable drive in which man thinks he will finally arrive at his ultimate freedom unfortunately is one more form of self-deception; because man is not and cannot be God. This desire inevitably leads to self-destruction akin to what we read in the scripture with reference to Adam and Eve being tempted to become like God. It was their desire to be like God, knowing

---

[86] *Jean Paul Sartre, Existentialism and Human Emotions – P. 84*

everything and being in control of everything, that lead to their fall and eventual eviction from the Garden of Eden (Genesis chapter 3). In Christianity this attempt or desire to be God which is done out of bad faith, deceived by the serpent, is sinful and leaves the individual with the feeling of guilt and the burdens that come with this guilt which includes a strained relationship with God.

It is in this light of man acting in bad faith that I see the assertion made by Jean Paul Sartre in his book *Existentialism and Human Emotions* when he wrote, "Man is the being whose project is to be God...To be man means to reach toward being God. Or if you prefer, man fundamentally is the desire to be God"[87] This 'reaching toward being God' is not a movement toward what I am attracted to, out of love, rather it is a movement borne out of rebellion. It is this rebellious mindset that is behind the event of Genesis chapter 11: 1-9, the Tower of Babel. The project of the tower was a total failure, in fact a disaster. And so is the man or woman who has set himself/herself the project of becoming God found out what a disaster this could be; the story of Frankenstein is there for all to see and learn from. Yet Sartre thinks that this is freedom for the individual.

The pursuit of the desire to be like God, to fill up every hole, from the Sartrean point of view is such an illusion that can only leave one very sad and unfulfilled. This takes us back to the original conclusion of Sartre that man's condition is forlornness, anguish and despair. It will eventually bring about the annihilation of the individual. Unfortunately Sartre regards this annihilation as equal to freedom, when he wrote, "Freedom in fact... is strictly identified with nihilation"[88] In other words, freedom means one losing one's being. This is meaninglessness in existentialist thinking and Paul

---

[87] *Ibid. P. 63*

[88] *Ibid. P. 65*

Tillich articulated this anxiety of meaninglessness in his book, *The Courage To Be,* and concluded that it is the necessary consequence of the "loss of an ultimate concern, of a meaning that gives meaning to all meanings"[89] In other words, one needs someone, a being whose meaning is assured upon whom one can anchor one's life for any veritable meaning. However for Tillich this is tantamount to one surrendering one's freedom, it is a sacrifice of the self in order to save oneself. He identifies the limitations in the freedom which human beings have as he analyzed the situation thus, 'meaning is saved, but self is sacrificed'. Eventually one in a bid to reassert oneself goes fanatical and even violent and intolerant; and the meaning which one originally sought and seemed to have found becomes of little or no value. To a certain extent I see what Sartre and Tillich are referring to especially going back to our earlier examples of children trying to fill up every empty space or hole, instances abound of kids who have been suffocated in so doing; there by losing their being. We all are used to sayings such as: 'freedom is not free'; 'freedom demands sacrifice', etc.

It is true that human nature is always striving for fullness, for happiness and above all for freedom. But yet humans must acknowledge that they can only go so far in their search and desire for freedom; these have to be sought within a finite frame. As Paul Tillich cautioned, "Finite freedom has a definite structure, and if the self tries to trespass on this structure it ends up in the loss of itself."[90] Human beings must know their limits; they must know when to let go and let God take control and give us the required direction. Unfortunately humanity has continued to tell itself that absolute freedom is possible and has gone ahead to set up structures

---

[89] *Paul Tillich – The Courage to Be, P. 47*

[90] *Ibid. P. 152*

which it judges to be adequate to provide this fullness and freedom. One typical instance is Marxism, but what came out of it? Paul Tillich gives us an insight, "It is the greatest tragedy of our time that Marxism, which had been conceived as a movement for the liberation of everyone, has been transformed into a system of enslavement of everyone, even of those who enslave others".[91]

VIII. Meaning and Values in Sartre

With the death of God, or do we say the non-existence of God, "there disappears with Him all possibility of finding values in an intelligible heaven. There can no longer be any good *a priori*, since there is no infinite and perfect consciousness to think it. It is nowhere written that "the good" exists, that one must be honest or must not lie, since we are now upon the plane where there are only men"[92]. This is the position of Sartre, a position that is shared by so many other atheistic existentialists including Nietzsche. It all means there are no objective norms, no preexisting values or a priori values by which an individual's actions or words are to be evaluated. In fact "it amounts to the same thing whether one gets drunk alone or is a leader of nations"[93] Against what or who do you measure the value of any of these actions? All these were previously safe guarded by a belief in an all knowing God who had them written down somewhere in heaven. But now the existentialist (Sartre) is convinced that this God does not exist, what next? How can man find meaning for himself without referring to a non-existent God? Uppermost in his (Sartre) mind must have been the consideration as to how man could be

---

[91] *Ibid. P.153*

[92] *J. P. Sartre, Existentialism is a Humanism – P.28*

[93] *J.P. Sartre, Existentialism and Human Emotions -94*

authentic. He maintained that there is no law-maker but ourselves, that we must decide alone, and that our liberation from forlornness will result from our decision not to seek outside of ourselves the goal of freedom.

Sartre being the unabashedly subjectivist that he is, enthrones man as the origin of all values, of course by the choices he makes. He wrote, "But ontology and existential psychoanalysis… must reveal to the moral agent that he is the being by whom value exists"[94] As it were there was/is nothing before man, nothing to look up to and nothing to rely on as one grapples with decisions and choices before one. This line of thought was endorsed by the humanist Paul Kurtz as James Barta cited him in his paper, *Bound to Earth: The Secular Humanism of Paul Kurtz*. According to Barta, Kurtz argues that meaning is a relational concept. It is a human creation found by "what we find in life and/or what we choose to invest life with." Since it is up to humans to define their own lives, courage is a central value. As Kurtz states, "no deity will save us; we must save ourselves."[95] Sartre had already given emphasis to this idea when he wrote earlier in his book, *Existentialism and Human Emotions*, "Before you come alive, life is nothing; it's up to you to give it a meaning, and value is nothing else but the meaning that you choose"[96] But isn't this a recipe for chaos, for the same words and actions could be good and bad at the same time depending on who chooses what? Obviously it is of more importance to Sartre to be consistently inconsistent in preaching the place and freedom of the individual than in realizing what a disorder his position could lead to in our universe. He is promoting permissiveness; anything goes mentality. He wants to do away with

---

[94] *Ibid. P. 94*

[95] *James Barta, Bound to Earth: The Secular Humanism of Paul Kurtz, P.7*

[96] *J.P. Sartre, Existentialism and Human Emotions, P. 49*

everything that held humanity together, of course he did not ascribe to a universal human nature, and there are no ideas written anywhere by which men's actions are to be measured.

To further protect his theory of man being the origin of values, he posited that we should repudiate the 'spirit of seriousness' because it promotes the existence of objective values. This, he thinks, is our way of being authentic, to realize that there is nothing except what we cause to be. If we were to follow his arguments, nothing, not even the being itself, could be taken seriously. But I must first find value in my own life for me to be able to make choices that will advance my life. The issue with Sartre is that even though he enthrones man as the source of all values, he does not see a lot of value in this 'man'. After all what is man for Sartre? For him "all human existence is passion"[97] It is a constant strife; a being in flux, constantly in pursuit of being – finally he is nothingness. And how can this nothingness, a being whose existence is forlornness, despair and anguish guarantee any values in itself when it doesn't even have a value? There is a Latin adage that says, "*Nemo dat quod non habet*" (no one gives what he does not have). How can man who doesn't even know the meaning and purpose of his own existence create meaning and purpose in this universe?

In spite of all his claims about the freedom of man and the ability of man to create meaning and values, as he wrote in '*Being and Nothingness*', "it (value) can be revealed only to an *active* freedom which makes it exist as a value by the sole fact of *recognizing* it as such"[98], yet he betrays his doubts in man's capacity when he later wrote in the same book, "...is it possible for freedom to take itself for a value as the source of all value, or must it necessarily be defined

---

[97] *Ibid. 92*

[98] *Jean Paul Sartre, Being and Nothingness, P.76*

in relation to a transcendent value which haunts it."[99] It seems after all that there is something that is out there before and beyond man (freedom, consciousness) which could be at the root of man's choices and actions. Could there be an absolute, transcendent value which Sartre is aware of and yet unable to ascribe to so that he doesn't undo the whole foundation of his philosophy of existence preceding essence? I am convinced that there is one and He is God; He is the one who can guarantee meaning and value in the universe because He created the world and has the master plan and purpose for which He created us. Since man was made in the image of God, man has dignity and worth, whatever the circumstances. In God, man finds meaning outside of himself. In the chapters ahead, I will elaborate on the place of this transcendent being, God, as the source and guarantor of true human freedom.

---

[99] *Ibid. P. 546*

CHAPTER 3

THE CONCEPT OF FREEDOM IN MORAL THEOLOGY

I.   The two concepts

Just as it is in the nature of human beings to seek happiness so it does belong to their nature to seek freedom and to act freely. Pinckaers underlined the importance of freedom to humans when he wrote: "Freedom is at the heart of our existence"[100] And it is true, for events in life have shown how much people resist any attempt to restrict their freedom. Yes, we are always seeking freedom, be it freedom from something (sometimes freedom from laws and obligations) or freedom to do something. Unfortunately though, there are many who equate freedom with license to do what they want and they end up causing harm to themselves and others in society. In an attempt to interpret the classical definition of freewill, we have been left with two main concepts of freedom and the moral theories that flow from each namely freedom of indifference (morality of obligation) and

---

[100] *Pinckaers Servais, OP- The Sources of Christian Ethics P.238*

freedom for excellence (morality based on happiness and virtue).[101] The former is an off-shoot of Nominalism rooted in the thoughts of the high scholastics, principally Ockham, and fanned into flame by Protestant ethicists, while the latter has its foundations on the thoughts of the Fathers of the Church and developed by St. Thomas and theologians of like mind.

With the coming of the Scholastics, principally St. Thomas Aquinas, Moral theology began to deal with particular issues such as human actions, virtues, habits/habitus, etc. He developed treatises on these very important elements in moral theology, including the role of the intellect, will, free will, sensibility, etc. St. Thomas in particular was always interested in identifying how these elements came together to work towards the satisfaction of man's ultimate desire for happiness, which effectively is a participation in the life of God. In his thought there was always a link between being a good, happy individual and being a person of faith. Unfortunately discussions on sins and vices preoccupied scholars and brought in a negative slant to moral theology, such that the notion was given that the science was about prohibitions and limiting of human freedom.

In this chapter which will be mainly a reflection on the work of Servais Pinckaers, O.P. titled *The Sources of Christian Ethics*, I will be exploring in detail the manifestations and implications of the two concepts of freedom represented by Ockham with the Nominalists on the one hand and Thomas Aquinas and the Scholastics on the other hand. It shouldn't be surprising if I tend to devote a lot of attention on the freedom of indifference since it is a tendency that seems to have permeated and dominated most of theological thinking in the modern era. It brought the treatise on freedom to the fore and relegated basic natural concepts such as virtues, *habitus* and

---

[101] *Ibid. p.239*

freewill to the background. It so stretched the nature of Freedom, both human and divine, that I am left wondering, what next? For instance when Ockham spoke of the indeterminate, infinite will of God suggesting that God could even will against himself: "Every will can conform to the divine precepts; but God can command the created will to hate him, and the created will can do this"[102] Suffice it to say that the notion of freedom of indifference has been with us since the period of the high scholastics and has apparently tainted most of theological thinking even up to this moment. The pull is so insidious, that a lot of unsuspecting theologians find themselves even roped into this tendency before they know what has happened. I will often interchange Ockham, Nominalism and freedom of indifference in the course of this chapter because in my understanding they are all partners in crime.

II.   What is Freedom of Indifference?

In Ockham's doctrine, "free will preceded reason and will in such a way as to move them to their acts. 'For I can freely choose, he said, to know or not to know, to will or not to will'"[103] With this assertion, freedom assumes a primary role; as it were it becomes the absolute. This has come to be known as freedom of indifference since the human will must always retain enough indifference such that it may never be determined by any outside influences, for if it is determined by anything outside itself, it is not ultimately free. According to this doctrine, the will was not bound by anything. It could choose evil if it wanted to, or it could choose good if it wanted that at the time. The emphasis for Ockham is on the will, and eventually there will be

---

[102] *Ibid. P.247*

[103] *Ibid. P. 331*

a clash between God's will and the will of the individual. It is about self-assertion and affirmation. The will could do away with reason if it so chooses; so what informs the will in making moral decisions? At this rate the individual could even impose his will on God, and why not will God out of existence?

The freedom to choose between evil and good is an essential element in the freedom of indifference. In his well celebrated work, *Freedom of the Will,* Jonathan Edwards argued that an 'indifferent will' not only seems to destroy freedom, but morality and responsibility as well. If an objective good is chosen indifferently, a morally good choice has not really been made: "if there be any acts which are done in a state of equilibrium, or spring immediately from perfect indifference and coldness of heart, they cannot arise from any good principle or disposition in the heart; and consequently, according to common sense, have no sincere goodness in them, having no virtue of heart in them."[104] It really doesn't matter what one chooses, the important thing is that one is freely choosing. It is a freedom to make mistakes with no qualms of conscience. There is no value judgments per se, may be stretched furthermore, everything is permitted. Need I remind anyone of the dangers of permissiveness? As long as a person is able to freely will his decisions and actions, he is expressing his freedom. My worry here is how do we safe guard the common good? How do we ensure that each person's expression of freedom does not violate another person's right? I was told once that a person's freedom to stretch his hands stops at the point that it gets to another person's face. How would the freedom of indifference respond to this existential reality? Probably it may say that might is right, just will through your freedom. This of course is a recipe for violence and confusion in society.

---

[104] *Edwards, Freedom of the Will, 54 col. A.*

a. Destruction and Division:

In my reflection on the freedom of indifference, I have little doubt in my mind that I see things from the same exact lens as Pinckaers. A neutral reader might say that Pinckaers was too harsh with Ockham and his disciples, but given the dichotomy and destruction their ideas introduced into moral theology, no adherent of the theology of the Patristic and Scholastic era would not bear grudge with Ockham. Ockham and the Nominalists who promoted this system of moral theory, in their quest to annihilate the moral structures that held humanity together could be compared to nihilists and the effects they had on philosophical thinking. Freedom of indifference has a destructive influence on morality as we had it from the Fathers of the Church. It destroys the harmony between nature and humanity; and leaves in its wake confusion and uncertainty. It enthrones relativism and doubt. Negation is the bedrock of freedom of indifference; it has in it such a passion to choose against positive, and this for it is the whole essence of freedom. Philosophy is all too familiar with Ockham's razor; well here comes that razor again slicing through the known contours of moral structures. The wound inflicted on moral theology by Nominalism is so deep that even today we are still struggling with the effects. It has left its imprint on modern society's attitude towards authority (civil, ecclesiastical or otherwise), scripture and by extension, divine law. Nominalism and Ockham in particular were perpetually in conflict with the church's position on a lot of moral issues; little wonder William Ockham was excommunicated from the Church by Pope John XXII, although the excommunication has recently been lifted.

b. Nominalism and Protestantism:

It has been suggested in certain theological quarters that probably the moral theories of Ockham and the Nominalists provided Protestantism some grounds for their later theological positions such as the distrust of natural inclinations, the notion of 'either...or', the separation of reason and will, the undermining of papal authority, etc. In as much as we may not have authoritative sources to draw such a broad conclusion, there are certainly some similarities in their theological thought pattern that could lend credence to such suggestions. The Protestant distrust of human nature would stand out as an area of agreement with freedom of indifference. Just as Ockham in his theory of freedom of indifference brought a rupture between humanity and nature, so did Protestantism create a rupture between faith and morals.[105] In the thinking of Protestant theologians, morals did not count for much, just as for Ockham, nature (which only existed in name) did not count for much. They could not see the possibility of the co-existence of two equally good realities. Their approach was always too simplistic; it had to be 'either...or'.

However let me quickly acknowledge that there are variety of areas where Protestantism, particularly Luther, differed from Ockham and the Nominalist theological theories. One of those areas would include Nominalists teaching on grace which tilted towards Pelagianism, in which they claimed that "human beings were able to love God perfectly without the assistance of grace". Luther decisively rejected this doctrine stating that he "found no authorization in St. Paul or St. Augustine for such a rosy view of human nature". Consequently he rejected all accounts of salvation

---

[105] *Pinckaers Servais, OP- The Sources of Christian Ethics, P. 282*

according to Ockham and the Nominalists[106]. This is not surprising to me and any close follower of Luther and Protestantism for that matter, after all work has no value; it is faith alone that matters. The only thing I find interesting is that Luther was being more Catholic than the disciples of Ockham who were mostly Franciscan monks. Suffice it to say therefore that even though the effects of Nominalism could be seen in the Protestant moral theories, it will not be completely correct to conclude that Protestantism is an off shoot of Nominalism. Protestantism just happens to be a victim of the insidious threat posed by Nominalism, as revealed prominently in freedom of indifference, to the modern era, a threat which some unsuspecting catholic moral theologians have already succumbed to. As Pinckaers pointed out: "Even among Thomists, freedom of indifference was accepted, though it had caused the relativism against which they were fighting"[107]

c. Destroy in order to build:

In speaking about the freedom of indifference, we are speaking about a freedom which always has to impose one thing over the other, as it were, destroying in order to build. It is a departure from the age old teaching of St. Thomas that grace builds on nature, not destroy it. It encourages the possibility of one choosing contraries, that is to say one is free to choose happiness or not, good or evil; in fact it is indifferent to nature. Pinckaers in exposing the thoughts of Ockham had written: "The harmony between humanity and nature was destroyed by a freedom that claimed to be 'indifferent' to nature

---

[106] *David C. Steinmetz, an article in The Christian Century, August 23, 2005, pp. 23 and 25.*

[107] *Pinckaers Servais, OP- The Sources of Christian Ethics P.352*

and defined itself as 'non-nature'"[108] This lack of harmony surely does not augur well for humanity and any concept of freedom that prides itself on disharmony and discontinuity must be dysfunctional. It negates the divine will and creates a divorce between the Creator and humanity. This is a freedom that encourages one to choose against oneself and one's eternal end i.e. happiness. As Pinckaers observed, "For Ockham, the state of being ordered to happiness, however natural and general, was subject to the free and contingent choice of human freedom"[109] For Freedom of indifference the act of choosing negative has become fun, mindless fun, but for me it is incoherent to say the least; it started off looking out for the individual and ended up debasing and ultimately depriving the individual of what is his deepest longing.

d. Freedom of Indifference and Scripture:

Freedom of indifference is also responsible for the distancing of moral theology from Scripture. This was a direct assault on the Fathers of the Church who had taught that "all of Scripture possessed a moral dimension and significance"[110] Sadly, freedom of indifference called into question, or should I say treated with utter disrespect any part of Scripture that did not contain moral imperatives. Any denigration of any part of Scripture amounted to the denigration of the whole of Scripture. As Raymond Brown had argued: "the meaning of the Bible is to be found not in isolated passages, but in the passage taken in the context of the entire book in question and ultimately of the entire Scripture"[111] In the Bible itself we read:

---

[108] *Ibid. P. 333*

[109] *Ibid. P. 333*

[110] *Ibid. P. 199*

[111] *Odozor P.I, Moral Theology in an age of Renewal, 2003, P.136*

"All Scripture is inspired by God and profitable for teaching, for reproof, for correction, and for training in righteousness, that the man of God may be complete, equipped for every good work"[112] In the light of this, why would the proponents of the theory of freedom of indifference pick and choose the parts of Scripture to accept and reject others? The Second Vatican Council, citing the encyclical of Pope Leo X111 *Providentissimus Deus*, came against this distancing of moral theology from Scripture tossed around by freedom of indifference when it taught that "Sacred Scripture should be, as it were, the soul of all theology"[113]

Ockham equated the authority of Scripture with that of the Church and since he had his misgivings about the authority of the Church, Scripture was not a big thing in his moral theory. The only part that mattered would be the part that contained moral imperatives and obligations such as the Decalogue. This is easily understandable because Ockham and Nominalism promoted the morality of law and obligation, doing away with the morality of virtues and the beatitudes. As is in his character, he took only what served his purposes and threw away whatever he considered irrelevant. By so doing Ockham created a canon within the canon of the Bible. I think Ockham and his cohorts should have made up their minds to either accept revelation in its entirety or reject it. They cannot have their cake and eat it. He destroyed the unity of the Bible and cast a big doubt on the authority of the Scripture as a whole.

It is true that there are so many issues that cannot be resolved just by looking at the Scriptures alone; nevertheless, I agree with the Fathers that the Scriptures should be a veritable starting point for the Christian in resolving moral issues. Let us not forget that Scripture

---

[112] *Cf. 2 Timothy 3:16-17*

[113] *Vatican II, Optatan Totius, no. 16, ed. Flannery P.719*

is the soul of theology. This point was also made by Pope St. John Paul II of blessed memory in his address to the youths of the three Venezias on Sept 12, 1982, as he said: "The Gospel does not present immediate solutions to problems, but enlightens man's mind to find the total meaning in life, of the person, of human values such as freedom, love, the family, work, culture..."[114]. In the opinion of the Fathers, an adherence to the Scriptures would help one attain the level of spirituality necessary for one to come to the desired goal of freedom and happiness on earth.

e. Freedom of indifference and the autonomy project:

At the root of freedom of indifference is the obsession of Ockham and his cohorts to place humanity at the center of everything. The autonomy project was "the claim that human beings are radically autonomous, self-creating "selves," whose primary relations to others are relations of power"[115] In the words of Pinckaers, "freedom of indifference was thus impregnated with a secret passion for self-affirmation, deeper than any of its manifestations and expressions"[116] Pushing this further meant that man could even assert himself over God, for Ockham this was self-affirmation. It all means that humanity was now in a position to decide right or wrong based on the choices each one made. "Freedom, for Ockham, has little or no spiritual character. The reality is autonomous man, not virtuous man, for freedom has nothing to do with goodness, happiness, or truth. Freedom is simply willfulness. Freedom can attach itself to

---

[114] *"L'Osservatore Romano", ed. English, October 11, 1982, p.10*

[115] *George Weigel, A better concept of freedom pub. in Catholic Education Resource Center*

[116] *Pinckaers Servais, OP- The Sources of Christian Ethics, P.339*

any object, so long as it does not run into a superior will, human or divine."[117]

With freedom of indifference came the enthronement of subjectivism. At the center of every decision and action was the individual's self-interest. Obviously it was this kind of concept of freedom that Thomas Hobbes was so worried about that he warned in his book, *Leviathan*, that if individuals within a society continually lived by their own self-interests, they would continue to hurt each other and be stuck in a "state of war." Hobbes advocated that all the various individual wills and self-interests be handed over to a sovereign authority, even though I do not agree with his notion of sovereign power; for the individuals can still come together at any point to take back their wills and hand them over to another sovereign power. Nevertheless, Hobbes recognized that there was always something wrong with allowing every individual to impose his will on others freely. Freedom of indifference craved autonomy for humanity and did away with any form of dependence, even dependence on God. This is a recipe for chaos in society, for each individual could make his own law according to his own choosing at any given instance. How can we ensure that the freedoms of others are respected without trampling on the freedom of this one individual? I think that the correct position should be that man's freedom is contingent on God who already willed it. St. Irenaeus had taught that 'God's glory is man fully alive', and of course man fully alive should be the man glorifying God. This way God is free and man is free too.

---

[117] *George Weigel, A better concept of freedom pub. in Catholic Education Resource Center*

III. Freedom for Excellence:

But yet there is another concept of freedom in moral theology, one supported by the Church Fathers and St. Thomas; it is identified as freedom for excellence. According to St. Thomas, "freedom is a faculty proceeding from reason and will, which unite to make the act of choice. ... Free will was not a prime or originating faculty; it presupposed intelligence and will"[118] Informed by reason, freedom perceives what is good, just and right; propelled by the will, freedom desires knowledge and happiness. For Aquinas, freedom is not the capacity to choose between contraries. The will is created to be inclined towards the good and so it simply cannot choose evil. Freedom takes in the big picture and positions itself in such a way that its choice does not do violence to the proper order of things. It asks the relevant questions such as: what ought a man created in the image and likeness of God do in a given situation? How does my choice enhance my nature as a member of the community of individuals? Does this particular action destroy or ultimately ensure my happiness? Of course it asks the question, is pleasure invariably equal to happiness? Reason provides the free will with the necessary information it requires in order to come to a correct answer to these questions and finally make decisions. Interestingly, only a truly free individual could go through this process, and this is freedom for excellence and it is this freedom that can satisfy the deepest desire of the individual to be free.

Freedom for excellence agrees more with the nature of humanity and has one of the principal characteristics of a living organism-growth (developing). It passes through different stages of growth until it arrives at maturity just as the individual. It operates within

---

[118] *Pinckaers Servais, OP- The Sources of Christian Ethics P. 331*

the individual, co-operates with the individual to help him avoid mistakes in his choices thereby enabling him to arrive at his ultimate goal, i.e. eternal happiness. It uses nature as a spring board to leap to the desired heights. It does not denigrate nature as is the case with freedom of indifference; rather it recognizes the liberating capacity of nature in enabling an individual to make right decisions. Virtue which Pinckaers defines as 'a personal capacity for action, the fruit of a series of fine actions, a power for progress and perfection,'[119] is the engine propelling the growth of this freedom in an individual. It develops over a period of time and is interiorized in the individual such that one continually chooses the good over evil at each point in life. This notion of continuity, and I dare say, consistency in choosing according to goodness and truth, is what is so lacking in freedom of indifference, and it is what makes freedom for excellence, in my judgment, proper for humanity which is a continuum.

a. Freedom for excellence and Discipline:

As I have already mentioned above, consistency in making right decision is central in freedom for excellence. In order to ensure this consistency, a certain level of discipline which comes from training is required of the individual. There is nothing arbitrary about this concept of freedom; the will is created with an inclination to the good and has to place itself in such a position that it is so well prepared to ensure that it chooses good over evil at each given time. Just like an athlete needs training in order to perform consistently at a certain level in sports, so would the individual require training with the help of moral educators in the formation of the 'principal rules of moral life'. Generally there is always difficulty involved in keeping

---

[119] *Ibid. P. 364*

71

up with the discipline involved with the formation of the requisite balance in the individual between personal freedom and law, and yet it is an exercise worth taking. We are used to the cliché, nothing good comes easy; at other times we hear it said, 'good things are not cheap and cheap things are not good'. Not that I subscribe to this later part entirely, but it's just to give an indication to how freedom for excellence requires some hard work whereas with freedom of indifference, it's like anything goes.

The freedom for excellence is geared towards making the individual, and by extension, humanity better. As Pinckaers observed, citing Father Laberthonniere, the freedom that the Catholic educator, moral theologian, must seek to encourage is "the freedom that does not give into self, but conquers self... One becomes free only by becoming better"[120] This is the freedom that puts everything into the right context, understands the interrelationship between the individual, society, the rest of creation and the Creator. It enables one to recognize one's responsibility in exercising one's freedom for his ultimate happiness, realizing that freedom is at its best when it helps one to be more connected with God and others in society. One who operates from this concept of freedom does not glory in disharmony and divisions; rather he is generous, truthful, just, loving and humble. It is obvious that the most important thing for this kind of freedom is increase in virtue and a never ending aspiration towards the good.

b. Freedom for excellence is a freedom to serve:

Only a person who has a sense of true personal freedom can serve another as a moral obligation. Pinckaers pointed out that "The perfection of moral freedom is shown by the response to a vocation,

---

[120] *Ibid. P. 361*

by devotion to a great cause, however humble it may appear to be, or the accomplishment of important tasks in the service of one's community, family, city, or Church"[121] Immediately my mind goes to Blessed Mother Theresa of Calcutta and other individuals of like dispositions, who would go out of themselves to take care of others without asking for what is there for them. One cannot but think about those first responders at the Twin Towers on 9/11 as individuals who understood what it meant to be free and how to use one's freedom. But yet imagine what a few others; the terrorists did with what they understood to be the exercise of their own freedom. It is in view of the understanding of freedom for excellence that the life of Jesus on earth would be presented as the manifestation of freedom par excellence. In the Scriptures we hear Jesus speak of the freedom he had to "lay down his life and take it up again" (John 10:17-18) and also we were encouraged by St. Paul to have the same mind that was in Jesus (Philippians 2:5-8). Freedom for excellence engenders humility and enables one to take his proper place in the order of existence and gives God his proper place, quite unlike freedom of indifference that sought to replace God in the name of self-affirmation or the 'autonomy project'.

c. Freedom for excellence and Grace:

It is through freedom for excellence that we can enter into any meaningful relationship with others and with God too. According to Pinckaers, St. Thomas was able to find a connection between the action of the Holy Spirit and the manifestation of personal freedom. Truly free individuals walk with the light, they don't hide from the light neither do they quarrel with the light (John 8:12). It is the

---

[121] *Ibid. P.366*

Holy Spirit that leads a truly free individual into union with God. In Thomas' words: "But the Holy Spirit moves us to act in such a way that he causes us to act voluntarily, in that he makes us lovers of God"[122] There is friendship and harmony between God's will and the free will of the individual, not disharmony and conflict as we notice in freedom of indifference. The grace of God builds on and elevates human nature, it does not destroy it. The union between grace and nature can only be for the good of nature, not detrimental to it. Karl Rahner underlined the importance of the relationship between grace and nature which he understood to be necessary. For him, "Nature must be if the divine self-giving is to have an addressee. Creation is grounded in God's gracing love. Nature exists for grace never apart from grace"[123]

St. Augustine had pointed out in 'his Confessions' that our hearts have been made for God and we are restless until we rest in God[124]. A man is truly free and happy when he submits his will to God, this is freedom for excellence. I cannot help but think about what happened in the Garden of Eden according to the account in Genesis chapter 3 when Adam and Eve chose to exercise their perceived freedom irrespective of the will of God. What level of unhappiness, shame and discomfort it brought to them, and eventually to the whole of humanity, until the obedience of Jesus changed all that. That goes to show what can happen when we choose against God in the name of freedom. The fate of those who are guided by the freedom of indifference could be likened to those St. Paul spoke about in Philippians 3:18-19, "their glory is their shame". Freedom comes from God and connects humanity with God. In a relationship with God

---

[122] *Ibid. P. 369*

[123] *The Cambridge Companion to Karl Rahner, P. 45*

[124] *St. Augustine, Confessions, P. 21.*

no individual remains the same. There is always an opportunity to change and become more Christ like. In our journey towards God, only freedom for excellence can enable us to develop our full potential with qualities of Jesus.

CONCLUSION:

From the foregoing, we can conclude that freedom is very essential for every individual, yet there are varied appreciations of the concept of freedom. Two major characters have been on display here (William Ockham and Thomas Aquinas), incidentally they were both monks: one a Franciscan, the other a Dominican. My humble assessment of the situation, especially in relation to the concept of freedom, is that Ockham came out as theological villain while Aquinas is the hero, and I am convinced that this too is the view of a majority of theologians today including Servais Pinckaers. I hope that in exploring the thoughts of Pinckaers in his book, *'The Sources of Christian Ethics'*, I have succeeded in making it obvious that there is a marked distinction between freedom of indifference and freedom for excellence. Freedom of indifference is a freedom to choose between contraries (good and evil) while freedom for excellence is freedom to choose the good; in fact for freedom for excellence the choice of evil is a lack of freedom. Freedom of indifference is indifferent or should I say, does violence to the nature of the individual, while freedom for excellence is rooted in the natural inclinations to the good and true. It might sound so simplistic and harsh, but the distinction St. Paul makes between the fruits of the flesh and the fruits of the Spirit in Galatians 5:19- 26 could be related to the distinction between freedom of indifference and the freedom for excellence. For St. Paul the fruits of the flesh include dissension, factions, selfishness, etc.; just as freedom of indifference is about disharmony, divisions, destruction, etc. On the other hand, he talks about the fruits of the Spirit to include love, generosity, self-control, etc.; do the hallmarks of freedom for excellence not include charity, service, discipline, etc.?

The concept of freedom promoted by Ockham and Nominalism which is freedom of indifference has brought more division and destruction to individuals and society. Placing humanity at the center of everything negates both God and morality. The things that have brought happiness and inner peace to humanity seem absent in the freedom of indifference. It promoted dichotomy between freedom and law, freedom and grace, and finally the subject and object. In reality I see freedom of indifference as apparent freedom. What good is free will if it brings destruction to others and hinders the growth of individuals who are constantly called to growth and transformation? Whereas freedom to do evil is essential in freedom of indifference, it is a lack of freedom in the freedom for excellence as Pinckaers submitted, "In freedom for excellence on the other hand, the ability to commit faults in our moral life as well as in the arts is a lack of freedom, lessened if not eliminated by progress"[125]. The dynamic nature and capacity for growth inherent in freedom for excellence encourage humanity to actively engage in paths and situations that will nourish growth: scripture, virtues, discipline, relationships, reflection and service. In this concept of freedom, even though there is still a temptation to do evil, there is an even greater desire to strive to choose good with the freedom we have received from God. We are always striving to become our best in the light of freedom for excellence.

---

[125] *Pinckaers Servais, OP- The Sources of Christian Ethics P. 376*

CHAPTER 4

FREEDOM AND GRACE

I. Exclusive Alternatives?

There are so many for whom the whole question of freedom is about what power and right each individual has to decide and choose his course of action without recourse to any external influence. In the light of this to speak of a relationship between grace and freedom breeds suspicion in their minds. For these individuals the two concepts seem to be exclusive alternatives. The problem has been stated variously as we have it in the *Catholic Encyclopedia*, "But is there not between these two principles an irremediable antinomy? On the one hand, there is affirmed an absolute and unreserved power in God of directing the choice of our will, of converting every hardened sinner, or of letting every created will harden itself; and on the other hand, it is affirmed that the rejection or acceptance of grace or of temptation depends on our free will. Is not this a contradiction?"[126] Elsewhere Montague Brown in an article in *The Saint Anselm's Journal* stated the argument thus, "For if we say that God's foreknowledge is absolutely certain, or that God is the cause of every activity, or that God's grace is necessary

<hr />

[126] *Portalié, Eugène. "Teaching of St. Augustine of Hippo." The Catholic Encyclopedia. Vol. 2. New York: Robert Appleton Company, 1907.*

for us to choose the good, then it is hard to explain how our choices can be free. On the other hand, if we claim that our choices are really free, it seems we must deny that God has any part in them, either knowing them with certainty or causing them".[127] But we can neither deny any. A close study of the teachings of St. Augustine will lead us to conclude that God is the cause of every action and human beings have freedom of choice.

II. The Providential Love of God

There seems to be a consensus among all right thinking theologians that there is always the need for divine assistance for humanity to accomplish anything that is noble, worthy and just. This divine help is understood to be 'grace'. Theologians in every age have variously defined the word grace, and to their credit, most have generously come up with very interesting notion of the word. In my reading of the *History and Theology of Grace* by John Hardon, S.J., one description of grace that caught my attention was when the author said, "instead of considering grace as a sporadic assistance or even as a static possession, we thus see it as a perpetual outpouring of divine benevolence,... as a dynamic power that God intends to have grow and mature under His providential hand"[128]. In other words, God is always involved with us each step of the way. And it is this understanding that leads me to think about the providential love of God, in which God extends his solicitous care to us. In his solicitude for us, God intended that through grace humanity be elevated to the divine life. It is not that we asked for it, in fact we had no right to this, it is gratuitous and unmerited. God simply decided

---

[127] *The Saint Anselm Journal 2.2 (Spring 2005) 51*
[128] *Hardon John, S.J., History and Theology of Grace, P. 7*

in his providential love to bestow it on us. As St. Augustine taught, 'Grace is the freedom of God to act without any external necessity whatsoever - to act in love beyond human understanding or control'.

How does God accomplish this? Grace is a Trinitarian reality; for God sent His only begotten Son, Jesus Christ, to become man in order to save us, and the Father and the Son sent the Holy Spirit to sanctify and preserve us. God is solicitous that all creatures attain their eternal end which is heaven and in His Son, Jesus Christ, He makes the means available. Every grace to will and do what is right has come from Christ and that is why he could say in the Scriptures, "Without me, you can do nothing" (John 15:5). And variously in the scriptures, and rightly so, Christ made absolute claims including when he said "I am the way and the truth and the life. No one comes to the Father except through me" (John 14:6). It is by his grace that we are saved. It is important to underline that Christ came not because we asked for him, but because God saw our need of salvation and wished to send us a Savior. So it is God who initiates and completes the work of our justification. God is the all provident Father who anticipates the needs of His children.

Unfortunately there are scholars ranging from Pelagius to the Rationalists of the enlightenment era who have suggested and even insisted that humanity is capable of willing and accomplishing what is right and just, and thereby ensuring their eternal goal of heaven without the help of the grace of Christ. John Hardon articulated and summarized their position when he wrote, "We can always will and do good, even when *de facto* we will and do otherwise, depending entirely on our own moral strength".[129] This is simply tantamount to pride that arises from what I will call a false sense of self sufficiency. Pelagius and his cohorts will do well to listen to the testimony of the

---

[129] *Ibid. P. 10*

Joint Commission of Lutherans and Roman Catholics as they wrote, "Together we confess: By grace alone, in faith in Christ's saving work and not because of any merit on our part, we are accepted by God and receive the Holy Spirit, who renews our hearts while equipping and calling us to good works".[130] There is nothing that we are or nothing that we have achieved that has not been because of God's providential solicitude towards us. St. Paul in his first letter to the Corinthians would ask, "What do you possess that you have not received?" (1 Cor. 4:7).

St. Augustine is rightly referred to as the 'Doctor of Grace' and among his many teachings on grace he outlined that every good work, even good will, is the work of God. His criticisms against the position of Pelagius on the individual's ability to will and act independent of God's grace are well documented. In his work *De gratia Christi 25 and 26,* he taught, "For not only has God given us our ability and helps it, but He even works [brings about] willing and acting in us; not that we do not will or that we do not act, but that without His help we neither will anything good nor do it."[131] In every discussion on grace, we must strive to maintain the delicate balance between God's providential care and the responsibility of the individual to cooperate with the grace of God. Here we are very grateful to the strong tenet of Catholic theology that it is always 'both and' (Grace and nature, faith and work, revelation and reason, etc.), as opposed to the Protestant doctrine of 'either or' (faith alone or work alone, scripture alone or Tradition alone, etc.). I think theology should always be about harmony, not disharmony. God pours out his grace on humanity in order to elevate us, not to humiliate us as some thinkers would want us believe.

---

[130] *Joint Declaration on the Doctrine of Justification P. 15*

[131] *St. Augustine, On the Grace of Christ and Original Sin*

To say that whatever we have received has come from God does not deny that humanity has freewill. One could resist or refuse to cooperate with the grace of God as John Hardon observed, "… By this act man offers to God Himself a free obedience since he concurs and cooperates with God's grace, when he could resist it"[132]. But still, one may ask the question, why should anyone in his right senses resist the grace of God? The grace of God can only make one better, not diminish an individual. Here the remarks of St. Augustine in 'his Confessions' that our hearts have been made for God and we are restless until we rest in God[133] becomes all the more pertinent. A person is truly free and happy when he cooperates with the grace of God. Ultimately God, through the infusion of Sanctifying grace and constant out pouring of Actual grace, is ensuring that we make choices that enable our journey towards our eternal happiness with Him. This grace is so sure of its results that human freedom will never in reality resist it, although it has the power to do so. For Augustine, there is no metaphysical necessity that the sinner respond favorably to grace. Yet it is certain that the sinner will respond to grace, for God's ability to woo an individual is such that he can convince even the hardest heart to repent. For Augustine, God's grace is infallible—it always accomplishes its purposes, but is not irresistible.[134]

III.   Powers and limitations of fallen nature

The reality called man is very complex in the sense that he could at one time be attributed with the noblest of characters and yet at

---

[132] *Hardon John, S.J., History and Theology of Grace, P.32*

[133] *St. Augustine, Confessions, page 21.*

[134] *Gerald Hiestand, Augustine on Grace and Freewill posted on the internet on July 10, 2006*

another time could sink to the depths of depravity in his actions. Among theologians there is an agreement on the issue that man was created with certain native rationality and will, but opinions and beliefs vary as to what happened after the fall of our first parents. Was nature fatally wounded that there is nothing good left? Does man still have free will? Can he freely know and will the good without help from God? In an attempt to provide answers to these questions, schools of thought have sprung up with very extreme views ranging from "Pelagians for whom free will is the only grace a man needs and ending, or rather continuing with those who despair of man's ability of himself to know any truth or do any moral good"[135]

The works of individuals like Pelagius, Caelestius and their disciples in their defense of how independent the free will is and how much man can accomplish without any divine help are well documented and I would rather postpone discussion on them for another paper. On the other extreme, of course, we have Jansenists who have so much extolled the role of grace that free will disappears. Neither would we spend so much time exploring the theologies of the Reformers who have argued that the fall so wounded and depraved humanity that the free will lost the capacity to do any good deeds. I will rather spend some time exploring the position of the Catholic Church which has maintained a middle ground on this issue. It should not be lost on anybody that the Church takes seriously the implication of the Incarnation- for Jesus is the 'proximity of God and the promise of man'. With Jesus, God is so close to us, and yet man has so much possibility. It is only by keeping our minds focused on Christ as God and man that we are confident about how God and man can act together.

It is the belief and teaching of the Church that the human mind

---

[135] *Hardon John, S.J., History and Theology of Grace, P. 48*

is capable of knowing some religious truth unaided by the grace of revelation, yet revelation makes for clarity of knowledge and facilitates the acquisition of the truth. Here the Church understands and accepts that revelation beams a clearer light on the object of our knowledge such that we become more certain of what we know. In other words, "Our minds are not so debilitated by hereditary sin that they cannot know anything in the suprasensible order without remedial grace from God"[136] There is always a natural longing in man to know and understand the good, which of course was planted by God in man from the moment of creation; and this he did not entirely lose by the reality of the fall of our first parents.

What is said of the mind could, even if in a lesser degree, be said of the will- there is still some essential goodness left in the natural will that man could still will and aspire towards the good and noble, antecedent of divine help. Here the teaching of St. John Chrysostom comes handy when he said, "We must first select the good, and then God adds what pertains to His office. He does not act antecedently to our will, so as not to destroy our liberty"[137] However, one must understand fully the context of this statement of St. John Chrysostom, so that we do not veer into the realm of the Semi- Pelagianism in which case we will interpret him as insinuating that an "unbeliever can by his powers merit supernatural grace to start on the pathway of heaven…"[138] Chrysostom, like St. Augustine, St. Thomas and other Fathers of the Church were unanimous in believing that grace elevates and builds on nature and not destroy it. It has even been observed, with a lot of care I must caution, by Guy de Broglie, S.J,

---

[136] *Ibid. P.81-82*

[137] *Ibid. P. 85*

[138] *Ibid. P. 53*

that St. Thomas taught that grace was "a perfection given to nature in the same direction towards which its own tendencies are working"[139]

It is very true that the Church has consistently held to the belief that even after the fall, there is still some intrinsic goodness left in the natural mind and will of man, yet the Church acknowledges that man has been sufficiently wounded that he will need divine help in order to know and will the moral good necessary for him to arrive at his eternal goal. There is always a consequence of the sin of our first parents; it just cannot be the same. By the event of the fall, humanity lost sanctifying grace and with it went the facility to obey the moral law and the capacity to persevere in just and noble actions. One of the very clear effects of the fall is the fact that it has become obvious to man that he is completely dependent on God, dependency on a continued basis which is manifested in frequent prayers offered by man to God. The good news is that we have a God who cares that much that He will not refuse us the help we ask for in prayers. And that is why Jesus taught us to refer to Him as 'Our Father' in the prayer that he taught us (Matthew 6:9-13) – a prayer that encapsulates all our hopes and desires as we strive toward our eternal goal which is heaven. Only God the Father, through the Son Jesus Christ, in the Holy Spirit, is able to ensure that we receive the necessary graces to know the good and strengthen the virtues in us to do what is right always.

IV. Sanctifying Grace

The understanding of the Church on the doctrine of Sanctifying grace otherwise known as Justification, traces its origins back to the teachings of the Fathers of the Church. The Fathers were of course

---

[139] *Henri De Lubac, The Mystery of the Supernatural, P. 24 (footnote #30)*

reflecting on the idea of the effect of Original sin and the impact of the Christ event i.e. his birth, passion, death and resurrection on humanity. There was no question in their mind based on the teaching of the apostle Paul in the Scripture (Romans 3:21-31), that God has justified and restored us in and through Christ His Son. But with the advent of the Reformers, along with their narrow and fundamental reading of the Scriptures, the Church felt compelled to devote more time and energy in enunciating more clearly and definitively the meaning of Sanctifying grace. This was dealt with chiefly by the Council of Trent held from 1546 - 1563. There wasn't really a question of whether man is justified or not, rather at issue was, what happened when a man is justified? Close to this question would be: what is the process of Justification? In response to both questions the Catholic Church and the Reformers went different ways. As an ardent Catholic, I feel very indebted to John Hardon, S.J. for the work he has done in his book, *History and Theology of Grace*. He has so well underlined the differences and I will briefly point them out in this discuss.

Justification is the forgiveness of sin which we receive through Christ. According to the Council of Trent, Justification is "a passing from the state in which man is born a son of the first Adam to the state of grace and adoption as sons of God (Romans 8:15), through the second Adam, Jesus Christ our Savior."[140] Justification means regeneration, renewal, reconciliation, etc. When one is justified one's sins are completely removed and one becomes a new creature (2 Corinthians 5:17), God pours into the individual the graces and gifts necessary to sustain the new life one has received. This is classical understanding of the Church on the sacrament of Baptism; it washes away original sin and makes us children of God. But the Protestants

---

[140] *Hardon John, S.J, History and Theology of Grace, P.129*

argue that when a man is justified, "His sins are forgiven in the sense that they are covered over and not imputed to him, while internally he remains a sinner. And the justice he 'acquires' is not his own as something inhering in his soul…"[141] Not only does this not help man enough, it portrays God as not being as generous as we have known Him to be. Why would God merely cover over our sins instead of obliterating them? Why would God give up so much (death of His only begotten Son) just to accomplish so little?

Sanctifying grace is an infused grace poured out by God into an individual to enable one live the divine life of holiness, love and justice. As John Hardon, S.J, observed, "A person in the state of grace, therefore, is already living the deiform life that elevates him to the divine family, and has only to wait until heaven to enter its glorious fruition."[142] This is possible because of the grace of Christ's passion and resurrection. This grace inheres in the individual permanently and forms the foundation for all his virtuous choices in life. Through this grace, the individual is disposed to cooperate with God in attaining the eternal goal of the beatific vision. In the words of St. Thomas, "He (God) infuses into them certain forms or supernatural qualities, through which they are gently and promptly directed by Him in order to obtain the eternal supernatural good to which they are destined."[143]

V. Sharing the Divine Life

Every form of religion recognizes that in one way or the other, there is a relationship between the divine and humanity. In articulating this

---

[141] *Ibid. P. 129*

[142] *Ibid. P. 149*

[143] *Ibid. P. 139*

relationship, different religions have gone from one extreme to the other, from anthropomorphism to pantheism, etc. But the Catholic Church recognizes that through the infusion of sanctifying grace, humanity shares in the divine life. God gratuitously gives to man what ordinarily is reserved to the divine nature. It must be underlined that we had no claim to this; it is given to us as gift from God. When it is said that we share in the divine life it means that we participate in the life that belongs to God without diminishing God or taking the place of God, rather we are enriched by what we have received from God. God is an inexhaustible well, the giver that continues to give. Out of His generosity He is constantly reaching out to man in order to bless and elevate him to the divine nature. John Warwick Montgomery framed the argument strongly in his article on '*The Freewill Issue in Theological Perspective*' where he wrote, "because the most important possible decision in life, that of entering into a saving relationship with God, does not have its ultimate explanation in man's freewill but rather in God's sovereign love, humans are given every reason not to exercise hubris in thinking that they can build towers of Babel so as to climb up to God by their own self-centered efforts".[144]

Further evidence of our sharing in the divine nature is our enjoying the status of 'divine sonship by adoption'. Through this adoption we now share in the divine heritage which is eternal happiness. Great things happen when God mixes with man. The Incarnation is our blessing, for in humbling himself to become man, Christ has made it possible for us to share in the divine life. John Hardon, citing the Encyclical of Pius XII, *Mystici Corporis* of 1943, observed, "It is the will of Jesus Christ, that the whole body of the Church, no less than

---

[144] *John Warwick Montgomery, The Freewill Issue in Theological Perspective published in Global Journal of Classic Theology, Vol. 8, no. 2*

the individual members should resemble Him."[145] This resemblance involves living the life of freedom, holiness, justice and love; and so did he invite us to "learn from him for he is meek and humble of heart" (Mt. 11:29). The resemblance to Christ will give us access to the knowledge of the Father, and enable us live as children of the Father. This is only possible through the infusion of the Sanctifying grace into our lives.

VI.   Actual grace and Free will

Drawing inspiration from the declaration of the Council of Orange in A.D. 529, theologians have come to agree that Actual grace is "the internal enlightening of mind and inspiration of will that God supernaturally infuses in the respective faculties."[146] At a given instance, God supplies the individual with the necessary help required to know what is good, to reject what is evil and choose what is good. So often this is in answer to our prayers and therefore always attributed to the merits of Christ, who told us to "ask anything in His name and the Father will grant it" (John 15:16). Buoyed by this promise, Christians even go as far as asking for material gifts from God such as good health, outstanding talents, good jobs, etc., and are quick to attribute them to God when they are received. So these too are Actual graces from God. In fact for a true Christian everything is grace, everything good is a gift from God. Whereas we speak of Sanctifying grace as permanent, inherent in the individual, consequently habitual, we understand Actual grace as immediate divine help to the intellect and will in order to perform salutary actions. This grace does not permanently inhere in the individual;

---

[145] *John Hardon, S.J, History and Theology of Grace, P. 190*

[146] *Ibid. P. 208*

it is given for a particular action and vanishes as soon as the action is completed. However the action performed is directed towards the eternal salvation of the individual. I dare to call it 'practical grace'.

Given the reality of the effects of the fall of our first parents, even after the justification of the individual, there still remain obstacles on our path in performing salutary acts without the help of God. Actual grace therefore is God's intervention on our behalf. God in His providence uses various events, circumstances and even other individuals (as St. Paul asked, how will they hear without someone to preach to them, Romans 10:14) as instruments to infuse the necessary grace in the individual to aid in the accomplishment of a salutary act. Just as everything is grace, so also for the Christian every situation provides an opportunity for God to pour out His gifts. The Christian sees difficulties and challenges as opportunities; he looks at every stumbling block as a stepping stone by the grace of God. It is in the light of this that classical writers on spiritual life have identified situations such as temporal afflictions and adversity, persecution, temptations, in fact suffering in general as all various means of God providing opportunities for His creatures to be infused with grace. And this is true, for how often have we seen individuals transformed for the better after horrific experiences of sickness and suffering in their lives. It brings out the best in the individual suffering and also reveals the best in other individuals – family, friends and all who assist the sick and suffering- and this is the grace of God in action.

As we read in the Scriptures, 'it is God's will that all men be saved and come to the knowledge of the truth' (1 Tim. 2:4), yet we know that man has the freedom to accept or reject God's offer of salvation. So in play here is the reality of God's loving plan and the choice of the individual through his freewill. However because of the goodness and justice of God, who does not wish anyone to be lost (Ezekiel

33:11), He is always reaching out to all, including sinners and offering them opportunity to accept His grace for their salvation. In other words, I agree with John Hardon when he observed that, "No matter how sunk in bad habits or far from the practice of virtue, everyone receives – at least now and then – enough grace to be converted."[147] My reading of the situation is that, be it as it were that man has freewill, but the will of God that all be saved is so paramount that God will constantly make available to every individual the necessary grace for salvation.

A further area of interest is in relation to those who do not believe in Christ, a group that unfortunately is very large. How does grace work with and for them? I think that this is rather complicated, and a simplistic answer will not be enough to resolve this issue. However, bearing in mind that most of this people are invincibly ignorant, and so often not willfully choosing against God, it is the belief and teaching of the Church that God in His goodness and mercy will not allow them to experience eternal punishment. At least Pope Pius IX thought so when he wrote, "we may not establish limits to the divine mercy but hold it as certain that those who labor in ignorance of the true religion, if that be invincible, will never be charged with any guilt on this account before the eyes of the Lord"[148]

The teaching of the Church on the relationship between God's grace and human freedom remains very clear: "God's free initiative demands *man's free response*, for God has created man in his image by conferring on him, along with freedom, the power to know him and love him. The soul only enters freely into the communion of love. God immediately touches and directly moves the heart of man. He has placed in man a longing for truth and goodness that only he can

---

[147] *Ibid. P. 233*

[148] *John Hardon, S.J, History and Theology of Grace, P. 237.*

satisfy."[149] It surely makes for a great exercise in theological inquiry to understand the relationship between grace and human freewill, but at the end of the day, the teaching of St. Augustine initially directed towards the Pelagians, "God so acts in us that we both will and do what He wills"[150] remains the cornerstone of understanding this relationship. An individual in whom 'Effective grace' is present and functional finds it impossible to resist doing what is good.

VII.   Efficacious Grace and Supernatural Merit

In every discussion on the topic of Efficacious grace we find ourselves immediately plunged into the relationship between grace and freewill. The issue got even more intriguing with the coming of the Reformers, as new questions also arose about the understanding of predestination in relation to grace and freewill. In an effort to clarify this question, there was a heated theological struggle between two major religious orders in the Church (Dominicans and Jesuits). These two Orders were represented by the ideas of Bañez and Molina respectively. My favorite author on the question of grace, John Hardon, S.J. briefly examined each of their teachings in order to point out their differences, yet at the end of the day he concludes with relevant Church authorities that there wasn't really anything worthy of outright condemnation in the thoughts of these two scholars. The words attributed to Pope Paul V points to this 'no victor, no vanquished' position of the Church authorities in this matter: "in treating of this question, neither side may condemn the position opposite to his own or charge it with any censure."[151] Both

---

[149] *Catechism of the Catholic Church #2002*

[150] *John Hardon, S.J, History and Theology of Grace, P.248.*

[151] *Ibid. P. 258*

Benedict XIII and Benedict XIV supported the position of Paul V. This however goes a long way to alert any scholar making any inquiry on the issue of Efficacious grace and freewill about the delicate nature of the issue in question.

Bañez in an attempt to explain the relationship between grace and freewill leaned heavily on St. Thomas' teaching on the First Cause and Prime Mover. Consequently he postulated that for man to perform a salutary act, he requires the operation of two different graces namely, Sufficient and Efficacious. In his understanding, sufficient grace "gives a man the power of doing something good; but in order to have him actually do well or rightly use this ability, he needs another more powerful grace."[152] Obviously this more powerful grace would be Efficacious grace which includes the guarantee of the free consent of the will of the individual. Whereas it is possible for man in his freedom to resist sufficient grace, it is impossible for him to resist Efficacious grace. However, Efficacious grace does not do away with man's freewill, rather it so conditions the will that the man destined for salvation can only choose according to the will of God. Following on the thought pattern of Bañez, I am thinking here that this grace creates a favorable condition for man to use his freewill positively to choose what is good, for after all man was created to be obedient to the Creator. Freedom as John Kelly observed after all is "free will put to good use."[153] Before Calvinists and other Reformers start to think that Bañez has formed an alliance with them in repudiating the freewill, let it be known that there is a world of difference between his teaching and theirs. "Calvin denied freedom and built a whole theological structure on this premise;

---

[152] *Ibid. PP. 262-263.*

[153] *Kelley, John Norman Davidson. 'Early Christian Doctrines, P. 368*

whereas Bañez and his disciples resolutely defended human freedom under the impulse of grace."[154]

Whereas Bañez speaks of Sufficient and Efficacious as two different graces, Molina and his disciples insisted that they were not different substantially rather it was only in the accident of the ineffectiveness or effectiveness of grace that we can speak of it as being merely sufficient or efficacious. In other words we should speak rather of inefficacious grace or efficacious grace. If man's freewill acts in consonance with the grace of God, then that grace is efficacious, but if he resists the grace of God, then that grace remains merely sufficient. For the Molinists, it is in the nature of God to bestow grace and in the nature of man, by his freewill to either conform to the grace or reject it. They were very intent on establishing the autonomy of God in conferring grace on His creatures and also building a wall of security around freewill. However they taught that God has the foreknowledge of what decisions the individual will make even before He confers the grace, yet He bestows the grace in His Absolute freewill. Opponents of this theory frowned at the perception that Molinism makes freewill superior to the grace of God; making 'the efficacy or inefficacy of grace dependent on the arbitrary choice of a created will'.[155] Congruism which is an offspring of Molinism readily came to its defense against its opponents when it concluded that "the difference between efficacious and sufficient grace depends not only on the will of man, but also on the will of God... His selective choice of congruous graces, conferred under conditions so favorable to their efficacy... vindicates the divine sovereignty over His creatures and guarantees the absolute dependence on His will..."[156]

---

[154] *John Hardon, S.J, History and Theology of Grace P. 267*

[155] *Ibid. P. 273*

[156] *Ibid. 275-276*

In summarizing his understanding of St. Augustine's position on the relationship between grace and freedom, Gregory Neal submitted, "for Augustine free will has a place in predestination only to the extent of an individual's ability to receive Co-operating grace and move toward the "perfect freedom" of Available and Effective Grace. It is in this closed cycle of sin-grace-freedom that freedom can find its function. Sin can only be cleared by grace, grace comes only to those whom God elects, and it is only through grace that the perfect actualization of freedom can occur."[157] In speaking of grace, the Church has always understood that when one cooperates with the grace of God and performs virtuous acts, there is a reward for the individual – Eternal life. So there is a relationship between Grace and Merit, yet there is a difference. As the Council of Orange (A.D. 529) taught quoting St. Augustine, "Reward is due to good works, if they are done; but grace, which is not due, must precede that good works might be done".[158] It is God who grants the grace needed to accomplish virtuous works, He is the one who makes a promise of reward to those who cooperate with His grace, and He is the one who freely rewards those who lived a virtuous life with eternal life. So everything comes from God and ends with God. As we speak of reward, we also speak of punishment due to our refusal to act in accordance with the grace of God. So we are only rewarded or punished according to how we use our freewill in responding to the grace of God. In the final analysis, how we use our freewill matters; this is the consequence of our rational nature.

---

[157] *Augustine's Concept of Freedom: The Dynamic of Sin and Grace, an article by Gregory S. Neal (1989)*

[158] *John Hardon, S.J, History and Theology of Grace, P. 286*

CHAPTER 5

FREEDOM IN CHRIST

I. The existential question

The issue of freedom of the individual is inexorably linked with the identity and dignity of the individual. In this section of my work, I intend to explore the identity and dignity of Jesus Christ with the aim of linking the freedom of every individual (especially Christian) to the person and ministry of Christ. I will be relying heavily on the input from the work of Schubert M. Ogden in his book, '*The Point of Christology*'. Christology, in spite of all the odds it has come against, has this onerous task of helping both the believer and the inquirer with making some sense of the mystery of the person of Christ and certain key events in the life and death of the historical Jesus. How do we understand the identity of Jesus as both God and man? How do we view the many claims and assertions attributed to Jesus in the Bible – I mean is he the predicate or the subject? Of course how we answer this has enormous implications for us as human beings and gives us an insight about God himself. In carrying out his mission for the salvation of humanity, was it in his capacity as God or man or both? Was his death on the cross a self-surrender or in obedience to God the Father? Theologians of all persuasions have had their say on this topic yet a lot still remain inconclusive.

However, the question of the identity of Jesus is so very important that we cannot leave it to Christology as it has been done so far to answer. A deeper reflection is required because in answering the question "who is Jesus" I must also seek answers to the related questions, "who is God" and "who am I". It is in the light of this that Schubert Ogden suggested that the Christological question is an existential question, "... namely, that ultimate reality and therefore our own authentic existence as men and women are none other than they are disclosed to us to be precisely through Jesus"[159]

The search for identity has been with humanity from the beginning of history and at each epoch, depending on the level of learning and the experience of the group, the identity of being and its preservation has been variously characterized. But no other set of thinkers has been more interested in this project than the ones we call existentialist, be they Philosophers, theologians or even atheists. Identity is about self-affirmation which Spinoza saw as a participation in the divine affirmation. Paul Tillich articulated the thoughts of Spinoza very well when he wrote, "Perfect self-affirmation is not an isolated act which originates in the individual being but is participation in the universal or divine act of self-affirmation"[160] The claims and assertions of Christ find its basis on the understanding Jesus had of his special relationship with his Father who is God; and it does make a lot of sense for us who share a common human nature with Jesus to find our identity and meaning in God as the first principle. Yet there are existentialists, principally the atheistic existentialists represented here by men such as Jean Paul Sartre who

---

[159] *The Point of Christology by Schubert M. Ogden, P. 27*
[160] *Paul Tillich – The Courage to be, P. 23*

thought otherwise. For Sartre, human identity does not come from God, indeed not from anything or being outside the individual, "Man is nothing else but what he makes of himself"[161] Unfortunately Sartre's analysis of what man has made of himself does not make for a happy reading for man ends up in anguish, forlornness and despair.

The Christological question which Ogden suggested has to be called an existential question will make further meaning when engaged as a religious question. This has become necessary because there are so many things which are not immediately clear to the human mind about the world and our existence. We sure need further clarification about God, the world and ourselves. But to get the correct idea we must ask the appropriate questions. Rather than just ask 'who is Jesus' it will be important to ask 'what does the person and work of Jesus say to us about who God is' and what is the meaning of the events of the life and ministry of Jesus to us – our identity?

In the answers we get from these questions we might finally understand that life is not all doom and gloom as Sartre forcefully painted the picture of man who is forlorn, anguish and despair. Hopefully it will be revealed to us that the whole question of Christ is a love story in which God shows how much He loves the world and his Son and reveals that we fulfill ourselves more when we submit to this God of love. God has a plan for human salvation built around one like us, Christ, who accepted his mission freely and generously. Surely this is what Ogden had in mind when he summarized that "what is finally at stake in any answer to it is indeed an answer to the question of God but only in the sense that it expresses an understanding at once of what alone is ultimately real and of what we ourselves are therefore given and called to be"[162] God does not

---

[161] *Jean Paul Sartre – Existentialism and Human Emotions, P.15*
[162] *The Point of Christology by Schubert M. Ogden, P. 27*

threaten or obliterate our self – affirmation contrary to the thoughts of people like Nietzsche who said that "The submissive self is the opposite of the self-affirming self, even if it is submissive to a God".[163]

II. Meaning of our existence

The human person is constantly in search of meaning; meaning of his existence, the meaning of every event in one's life (including his actions and inactions) and the meaning of every religious assertion he makes or one that is made on his behalf. This was no different for the historical Jesus who is the subject of all Christological assertions. But at issue here is not only questions about this subject Jesus, as Ogden observed, "it asks about the meaning of Jesus for us here and now in the present, not about the being of Jesus in himself then and there in the past"[164] For the Christian it is very important to understand the underlying meaning of every Christological assertions made of Jesus since it is of existential consequence to every individual believer. Given the way he spoke and what he did, it is obvious to every observer, believer and unbeliever alike, that the historical Jesus was an embodiment of some special relationship with the ultimate being – God, and therefore in articulating the meaning of his (Jesus) existence and relating with him, every Christian finally would have overcome the anxiety of meaninglessness that seem to permeate our existence. As we have already observed elsewhere, Paul Tillich articulated this anxiety of meaninglessness and concluded that it is the necessary consequence of the "loss of an ultimate concern, of a meaning that gives meaning to all meanings"[165] In other words, one

---

[163] *Paul Tillich – The Courage to be, P. 29*

[164] *Schubert M. Ogden – The Point of Christology, P. 41*

[165] *Paul Tillich – The Courage to Be, P. 47*

needs someone, a being whose meaning is assured upon whom one can anchor one's life for any veritable meaning. However for Tillich this is tantamount to one surrendering one's freedom, it is a sacrifice of the self in order to save oneself. He identifies the limitations in the freedom which human beings have as he analyzed the situation thus, 'meaning is saved, but self is sacrificed'. Eventually one in a bid to reassert oneself goes fanatical and even violent and intolerant; and the meaning which one originally sought and seemed to have found becomes of little or no value.

But Christianity understands this differently for Christ had taught that his follower has to be prepared to lose himself/herself in Him (Christ) in order to save his/her life (cf. Mt. 10:39 and Mt. 16:24-26). We do not become less by submitting to Christ rather we become fuller and better. His teaching on the beatitudes in Mt. 5:2-12 is a very clear example of how embracing the qualities that Christ held up (qualities grounded on the Christological assertions which Christians have come to accept in faith) could give one a better meaning of one's existence. St. Paul also brings out this idea of self-emptying which Christ taught us by his own life as is recounted in Philippians 2:6-11. However, those who profess and tend to exercise their freedom without any reference to Christ as the source of the meaning of their lives, do often discover that they can only go so far. I am referring to the picture that Sartre captures very well when he wrote, "In this sense the responsibility of the for-itself is overwhelming since he is the one by whom it happens that there is a world; since he is also the one who makes himself be, then whatever may be the situation in which he finds himself, the for-itself must wholly assume this situation with its peculiar coefficient of adversity, even though it be insupportable"[166] Here there is nothing else to cling to, no one to

---

[166] *Jean Paul Sartre – Existentialism and Human Emotions, P. 52*

look up to and no one to hope in for solution to one's situation. This is despair, anguish and forlornness all over and eventually one may choose to end it all through suicide.

It is true that the debate still goes on as to whether the historical Jesus did actually make the Christological assertions upon which the Christian has pinned the meaning of his/her life or if in fact it was his witnesses (Christians) who are advancing these assertions based on what has been recorded in the synoptic gospels, however there seem to be a growing consensus among theologians about the importance of the historical Jesus in the quest for meaning for the individual. To insist and purport to establish that the historical Jesus never existed or that the witnesses lacked understanding of the Christological assertions they made would represent a very significant threat to the faith system of the individual Christian and as Paul Tillich rightly pointed out, "the threat to his *(one's)* spiritual being is a threat to his *(one's)* whole being"

The underlying idea that makes sense to me, which Schubert Ogden and several other scholars have ascribed to, is that every human being is longing for meaning into his/her existence, and this meaning could only be found in the ultimate reality – God, and it is not just about what God has said and done in the past, it is more about what God is saying and doing here and now in our lives. This meaning is found in the Christological assertions which Ogden insists "were all assertions about Jesus as the decisive re-presentation of God and, therefore, as the one through whom the meaning of ultimate reality and authentic understanding of our existence are made fully explicit"[167]

---

[167] *Ibid. P. 59*

III.   Self understanding

Immanuel Kant's rallying cry during the period of Enlightenment was "Dare to know" in which he encouraged humanity to make the required effort to know what could be known, especially to know what capacity the individual had and who the individual human person really is. It is true that this period made searching for knowledge and understanding a key point in human history, but the question of seeking and arriving at self-knowledge has been with humanity for a very long time. Unfortunately in some instances, individuals have been led by some extremist philosophical and theological scholars, scientists, humanists, atheists, and even the media to come to an exaggerated conclusion of who they think we are as human beings and what capacity they think we have such as when Jean Paul Sartre wrote that "Man being condemned to be free carries the weight of the whole world on his shoulders; he is responsible for the world and for himself as a way of being"[168] Sartre takes his understanding of human capacity and freedom too far such that he enthrones subjectivism over the Universal. I think it is a distorted understanding of the human person; one which even Sartre himself had to admit has brought the individual so much stress and discomfort. Paul Tillich in his book, *'The Courage to Be'* presents a better picture when he wrote, "Man lives in meanings, in that which is valid logically, esthetically, ethically, religiously. His subjectivity is impregnated with objectivity"[169] The human person has to understand himself/herself in relation to the Ultimate reality – God.

This authentic way of self-understanding has been identified

---

[168] *Jean Paul Sartre – Existentialism and Human Emotions, P. 52*

[169] *Paul Tillich – The Courage To Be, P. 81-82*

in Jesus as we explore the essential claims made of Jesus in the Christological assertions by his witnesses as Ogden pointed out, "Jesus is what the Christological assertion asserts him to be because, but only because, he is the one human being who consistently understood his own existence in the authentic way in which all human beings are given and called to do"[170] Through his obedience to God and his love and sacrifice for humanity, he reveals God to us (he re-presents God to us) and makes explicit to us what should be the authentic understanding of ourselves in relation to God. He taught us that humility was a virtue that was proper to humans in our relationship with God: thus he did not count equality with God something to be grasped (Philippians 2:6), neither did he claim absolute knowledge e.g. about the end of the world (Mt. 24:36). In this he becomes our model; he teaches us how to be in relationship with God and how we are to act in relation to our fellow human beings. For us to be authentic individuals, we have to be in relation both with God and other human persons. It was about this fact that Paul Tillich was writing when he said, "Only in the continuous encounter with other persons does the person become and remain a person"[171] He might not have mentioned here explicitly about being in relationship with God, but obviously he was establishing the fact that no one can have a self-understanding that does not look beyond oneself.

One of the deepest longing of every individual human person is the need for affirmation, and in the story of the historical Jesus as told in the gospels (Baptism -Matthew 3:17 and Transfiguration Matthew 17:5b), we have the testimony of God affirming him as his beloved son. This testimony readily speaks to our existential condition because we would easily see in the affirmation of Jesus

---

[170] *Schubert Ogden – The Point of Christology, P. 65-66*

[171] *Paul Tillich – The Courage To Be, P. 91*

our own affirmation as Disciples of Christ. The God who has such a loving relationship with His only begotten son is our God and Father (His adopted sons and daughters) and he is the one who has authorized our existence. To predicate the Christological assertions to the historical – existential Jesus is of enormous importance to my being and my faith in as much as it enables me to have some explicit image of who God is and also understand who I am called to be in my relationship with God and my fellow human persons.

IV. Authentic Freedom

Unfortunately humanity has continued to tell itself that absolute freedom is possible and has gone ahead to set up structures which it judges to be adequate to provide this fullness and freedom. One typical instance is Marxism, but what came out of it? Paul Tillich gives us an insight, "It is the greatest tragedy of our time that Marxism, which had been conceived as a movement for the liberation of everyone, has been transformed into a system of enslavement of everyone, even of those who enslave others".[172] Simply put, human beings cannot adequately provide and guarantee absolute freedom for themselves, it has to come from a being that is absolute – the Ultimate reality, who is God. It is high time humanity stopped being in denial and face up to the reality.

While absolute freedom is impossible for the human person, we can arrive at authentic freedom. This is to be found in Christ who is the power and presence of God and the promise and possibility of humanity. In the two natures (divine and human) united in the person of Jesus Christ, the image of God is revealed and all that the human being is called to be is revealed. The whole essence of the

---

[172] *Ibid. P.153*

witness of the Apostles is to demonstrate that Jesus makes explicit to us what is ultimately real about God and that faith in this God revealed by Jesus will bring us to what is authentically possible to us as human beings (cf. Ogden 87-88). In the gospel according to John in chapter 8:31-36, he articulates the importance of the individual holding on to Jesus and his word, because this is the truth that can set one free. He concludes the passage by asserting "If the Son sets you free, then you will be truly free".

Our freedom must have content; it cannot be empty or a license to do what we want or what we like. Freedom is to be found in truth and justice. This is necessary for the orderly functioning of the world; to preserve the relationship between the Creator and the creatures and to foster a proper relationship between human beings and the other creatures including the environment. This is the only freedom that could be meaningful otherwise human beings will sink into despair. It is this despair that some philosophical systems such as atheistic existentialism have been pushing humanity towards. But thanks to Christianity we are able to aspire towards authentic freedom in Christ as we read in St. Paul's letter to the Galatians, "For freedom Christ set us free; so stand firm and do not submit again to the yoke of slavery" (Gal. 5:1). In the witness of the early Disciples of Christ and in the courageous (in truth and justice) witnessing of all authentic Christians today we have the content of human freedom.

V. Called to freedom

John Sachs observed that God created humanity to be free when he wrote, "According to the Scriptures, in creating the world out of love in order to be its lover, God made a partner not a puppet"[173] God

---

[173] *John R. Sachs, The Christian Vision of Humanity, P. 28*

left humanity with responsibility for what he will become. However this freedom is not a license for one to do whatever one liked, rather it is the capacity to make choice, of course making the right choices. In his freedom one ought to put everything into the right context, understand the interrelationship between the individual, society, the rest of creation and the Creator. Freedom enables one to recognize one's responsibility in exercising one's freedom for his ultimate happiness, realizing that freedom is at its best when it helps one to be more connected with God and others in society. One who operates from this concept of freedom does not glory in disharmony and divisions; rather he is generous, truthful, just, loving and humble. It is obvious that the most important thing for this kind of freedom is increase in virtue and a never ending aspiration towards the good.

God in his infinite love created humanity with freewill. However in the consciousness of our freewill, we have equated freedom with absolute power and consequently we have gone all out to seek to acquire absolute power. It was this very desire that the serpent played on in the account of the 'fall' recorded in Genesis chapter three and put it in the mind of Adam and Eve that they could be God. Here comes the first instance of the misuse of freedom that will have to live with humanity. Humanity still had to take another shot at being God or like God (and make a name for itself) when they conspired to build the Tower of Babel in Genesis 11:1-9. The result of this ill-advised adventure is well documented in the scriptures. You would think humanity would step back, but the push still continues as Sartre wrote, "Man is the being whose project is to be God"[174] Yet at each point man confronts his limitedness and realizes how impossible it is for him to be the absolute being that he craves for. Humanity is consequently left with a sense of meaninglessness and despair;

---

[174] *Jean Paul Sartre – Existentialism and Human Emotions, P. 63*

then what is the fate of humanity? How can we authentically fulfill ourselves as human beings? Or let us ask the question as Paul Tillich did, "How is the courage to be possible if all the ways to create it are barred by the experience of their ultimate insufficiency? If life is as meaningless as death, if guilt is as questionable as perfection, if being is no more meaningful than nonbeing, on what can one base the courage to be?"[175] Would despair and meaninglessness constitute the final word in the fate of the human being created in the image and likeness of God, called to fullness of life and freedom?

For Christians our true freedom is to be found in Christ. As Ogden well-articulated it in his book, "the Jesus who means love and therefore, also means freedom, because being the gift and demand of God's love made fully explicit, he is the decisive re-presentation of our own possibility to be truly free"[176] This Christ is our hope of life and immortality; he is our liberator from forlornness, anguish and despair. He teaches us how to find our true selves in emptying ourselves and being submissive to the will of God (Philippians 2:6-11). If we empty ourselves as he did, then we will be elevated by God who can never be out done in generosity. He reveals to us the infinite love of God and shows us that it is possible for us to participate in the divine attribute which is love. As we are called into God's infinite love, we are also expected to replicate this boundless love to all of humanity irrespective of nationality, race, language or gender (cf. Galatians 3:27-28; Colossians 3:11). It is only by doing so that we will find meaning in life and be truly free, as Ogden summarized it, "to accept God's love through faith is to be freed from oneself and

---

[175] *Paul Tillich – The Courage To Be, P. 174-175*
[176] *Schubert Ogden – The Point of Christology, P.125*

everything else as in any way a necessary condition of meaningful life"[177]

We are the great beneficiaries of God's immense love: First we were created out of love; God willed humanity into existence out of his love and empowered us (Genesis 1:26-31). Secondly God reached out to save humanity through his Son Jesus Christ out of his love: "For God so loved the world that he gave his only Son, so that everyone who believes in him might not perish but might have eternal life" (John 3:16) and again scripture says, "In this way the love of God was revealed to us: God sent his only Son into the world so that we might have life through him" (1 John 4:9). Consequently for us to fully realize ourselves, or if we are to be true to our identity, we must practice love as we have been loved (1 John 4:11). Love drives away the negative feelings of fear and guilt; it conquers all things including despair, anguish and death. Love frees us from ourselves and enables us to live for others just as Jesus did. This is the true freedom; one which recognizes my freedom from fear and propels me to look out for the freedom of others as well. This is the freedom which Christ re-presented to us in his discourse on the Good Shepherd in John's gospel chapter 10. This is the freedom that truly liberates; this is the freedom that Christ the liberator gives. This is the freedom for which we were created and which truly gives meaning to our existence.

VI. The implication of the freedom we have in Christ Jesus

The Jewish people had a very interesting understanding of the promised Messiah; he was the one who would come to set them free from the Roman occupiers. So when Jesus appeared on the scene and was being talked about as the Messiah, hopes of imminent

---

[177] *Ibid.123*

liberation were raised among the people. Of course when he went to the synagogue in Nazareth and read out the prophecy of Isaiah, "The Spirit of the Lord is upon me, because he has anointed me to bring good tidings to the poor. He has sent me to proclaim liberty to captives … to let the oppressed go free …" (cf. Luke 4:16-19), he left no one in doubt on that particular day that he might truly be the one they had been waiting for, and that was why all eyes were fixed on him. But as events would unfold in the life and ministry of Jesus the people came to see that they had a rather wrong image of the mission of Jesus. The Romans remained in Jerusalem long after Christ came, and in fact they were the ones who supervised his crucifixion. Does this then mean that Christ is not the liberator; that he has not come to give us freedom? Is it to say that to be free in Christ has nothing to do with fighting for and expecting physical and material freedom? Was he wrong to claim that knowing the Son and believing in Him was the way to true freedom (John 8:36)?

In Galatians 5:1 we read, "For freedom Christ set us free; so stand firm and do not submit to the yoke of slavery". What is this freedom that we have in Christ Jesus? For sure we cannot equate this freedom with the freedom that social politicians are advocating for i.e. freedom from want, ignorance and oppressive government. Yet it is not the freedom that means we are unconcerned with the activities of our society as the theologian Reinhold Niebuhr indicated, "Christians simply as such have a political responsibility for the good order and justice of our civil community"[178] The freedom that Christ gives us is the one that liberates us from ourselves, from our selfishness, misconceptions and other vices that could be found in the individual, and disposes us to be obedient to God's will and design which will most often ask us to be of service to the brothers and sisters. It is the

---

[178] *Ibid. P. 156*

freedom that equips the individual by strengthening our faith which according to Niebuhr "…by which we can seek to fulfill our historic tasks without illusions and without despair"[179] In Christ we are set free from the bondage of fear, sin and guilt. A Christian is called away from superstition, error, deception, depravity, ignorance and a destructive life, from being a captive of Satan and facing eternal death. The freedom to which Christ calls us is not the license to do what we want which most of the time leads us to self-destruction and causes pain and unnecessary suffering to others.

The freedom we have in Christ is the freedom of love; the openness to receive the boundless love of God and willingness to express this love to others. Unfortunately the atheistic existentialists especially Sartre would not understand this freedom, for he had wondered if acknowledging such transcendental value was not an issue with human freedom when he asked, "…must it (*freedom*) necessarily be defined in relation to a transcendent value which haunts it?"[180] While Christ sets us free in order to feel at home with the transcendent, Sartre and his friends present us with a freedom that makes us suspicious and apprehensive of the transcendent. The obvious outcome of the existentialist attitude is that we pretend that we are free yet everywhere in chains; and that's why Sartre concluded that there is so much despair and anguish.

The Christian anthropologist, John R. Sachs raised a very important point when referring to the life of Christ, he asserted 'that true freedom is not merely freedom from', but rather 'it is a freedom for'[181]. Yes, it is a freedom for service. Only a person who has a sense of true personal freedom can serve another as a moral obligation.

---

[179] *Ibid. P. 157*

[180] *Jean Paul Sartre – Existentialism and Human Emotions, P. 95*

[181] *John R. Sachs, The Christian Vision of Humanity, P.33*

Servais Pinckaers had pointed out that "The perfection of moral freedom is shown by the response to a vocation, by devotion to a great cause, however humble it may appear to be, or the accomplishment of important tasks in the service of one's community, family, city, or Church"[182] It is when we can freely give of ourselves, our time and talents to others and to enhancing creation that we can truly fulfill ourselves. It is very essential for every individual that there is something or someone beyond the self that we relate to in order to feel alive, after all to be is to be in relation with. My involvement with the world would help me to satisfy the desire in me to be a partner with God in creation and recreation.

There are those among Christians, who would want us believe that the freedom we have in Christ does simply imply political responsibility to fight against injustice and inequality; while some others portray a Christian pessimism towards political revolution, for them freedom is about 'the rule of God in our hearts'. However it is important to underline immediately that it is not a question of 'either or' rather it is a 'both and' attitude that will suffice here. The rule of God in our hearts which comes from faith in Christ as 'the real presence of the liberating love of God' would inevitably lead us to get involved with the political struggle for the liberation of all those who suffer want and injustice in our society. The freedom we have in Christ is holistic and the activities emanating from this freedom has to be equally holistic, i.e. it has to address every aspect of the human person including his environment. The Christian who is conscious of his/her freedom in Christ must work to positively affect the affairs of the human society; this is what it means to be a disciple of Christ, this is what it means to witness to Christ the liberator of humanity.

It is in the light of this understanding that I find the thoughts of

---

[182] *Pinckaers Servais, OP- The Sources of Christian Ethics, P. 366*

the delegates at the General Assembly of the Catholic Church very instructional when they wrote, "The salvific mission of the Church in relation to the world must be understood as an integral whole. Though it is spiritual, the mission of the Church involves human promotion even in its temporal aspects. For this reason the mission of the Church cannot be reduced to a monism, no matter how the latter is understood. In this mission there is certainly a clear distinction–but not a separation–between the natural and the supernatural aspects. This duality is not a dualism. It is thus necessary to put aside the false and useless oppositions between, for example, the Church's spiritual mission and "diaconia" for the world".[183]

---

[183] *The Final Report of the 1985 Extraordinary Synod*

CHAPTER 6

FREEDOM FROM MILITATING CONDITIONS

In Christianity our notion of freedom extends beyond the here and now. It is not just about material freedom; it includes our spiritual freedom and speaks of eternal freedom. As the Scottish missionary, Rev. Andrew Murray wrote, "To be free, then, is the condition in which anything can develop itself according to the law of its nature, that is, according to its disposition. Without freedom nothing can attain its destiny or become what it ought to be. This is true alike of the animal and man, of the corporeal and the spiritual"[184]. St. Paul so well nuanced this understanding as he wrote to the Romans: "For creation awaits with eager expectation the revelation of the children of God; for creation was made subject to futility, not of its own accord but because of the one who subjected it, in hope that creation itself would be set free from slavery to corruption and share in the glorious freedom of the children of God" (Romans 8:19-21). In the theology of St. Paul there were certain conditions that he identified in humanity that he considered militating conditions from which humanity needed to be freed. Among the many conditions he

---

[184] *Andrew Murray, The New Life, chapter 49.*

emphasized sin, death, law, and flesh (body). This is echoed by Rev. Andrew Murray as he wrote in his book, *The New Life,* "The power of sin over us, the power of the law against us, the power of the law of sin in us, hinder us. But he that stands in the freedom of the Holy Spirit, he that is then truly free, nothing can prevent or hinder him from being what he would be and ought to be"[185]. St. Paul developed the thesis that freedom and victory over these factors would only be assured in Christ Jesus. I would like to explore further this thesis of St. Paul.

I.   Freedom from Sin

From the beginning, according to the creation account in the book of Genesis, there was perfect harmony between God and human, such that God even took a stroll every now and then to visit with Adam and Eve (Genesis 3:8). But this perfect harmony was broken when humans chose to disobey God. This disobedience is at the root of what we call sin, and humans began to hide from God. Most theologians agree that this primary sin of disobedience has as its result the reality of concupiscence, which is both a punishment for sin and the urge to sin. Sin is an offence against God. It is in the words of John Sachs, "a transgression of a divine command, rebellion against God and God's authority".[186] Let us be clear about this, Pope John Paul II insists, "clearly sin is the product of man's freedom"[187] He continued to describe sin as "the disobedience of a person who, by a free act, does not acknowledge God's sovereignty over his or her life, at least at that particular moment in which he

---

[185] *Ibid.*

[186] *John R. Sachs, The Christian Vision of Humanity, P. 60*

[187] *John Paul II, Reconciliation and Penance, #14*

or she transgresses God's law"[188] With sin, humans chose to turn away from God, refusing to acknowledge God as the source of their existence and in the process posit themselves as their own gods. In so doing man has upset the relationship which should link him to God and broken the right order that should reign within him. The result of this, says Fr. Thomas Pazhayampallil, S.D.B, is that "the whole life of men, both individual and social, shows itself to be a struggle, and a dramatic one, between good and evil, between light and darkness"[189] By sinning humanity has betrayed its essential vocation and lowered its dignity. Humanity lost its freedom and rolled into slavery.

Sin has both personal and communal/social dimensions. John Sachs rightly uses the teaching of St. John Paul 11 (Pope) as he cites a text from his Apostolic exhortation on Reconciliation and Penance given in 1984 to buttress this point when he wrote, "Every sin, even the most intimate and secret one, the most strictly individual one has repercussions on the whole human family"[190]. This is especially true when we realize that there is such interdependence among human beings and even non-human life, and a failure by one individual to act responsibly could have enormous consequences on the entire community. The saintly Pope was so much into the issue of the solidarity among humanity that he also drew our attention to the converse effect of the success of one individual or some individual members of the human community such as the saints using the words of Elizabeth Leseur, the French writer who had observed, "every soul that rises above itself, raises the world"[191] In the light of this, think of the harm that the adultery of a father or mother

---

[188] *Ibid. #14*

[189] *Thomas Pazhayampallil, Pastoral Guide, Vol. 1, P. 190*

[190] *John R. Sachs, The Christian Vision of Humanity, P. 63*

[191] *John Paul II, Reconciliation and Penance, #16*

which leads to divorce in a marriage could cause to the children in the family. How often do we see dysfunctional individuals being products of dysfunctional families and how does this translate to the larger society of human race? How about the silence of the powerful nations in the face of injustice and brutality meted out to the poor and defenseless?

All over scripture references are made of sin under various images including a) disobedience of God (Deuteronomy 28:15-17), b) despising God (2 Samuel 12:10), c) slavery (John 8:31), d) rebellion (Isaiah 1:2-4) e) pollution (Isaiah 24:5). Several theologians are unanimous in their agreement on the fact of the universal effect of sin on humanity, an agreement which Francis Pereira highlighted in his book, *Gripped by God in Christ*, as he wrote, "Sin is woven into the very texture of humanity as we know it, it is like a universally polluted, diseased, air which every human being breathes". He continued citing A.M Hunter, 'It is a universal, though not total corruption of man's heart'. Furthermore he would cite J.A.T. Robinson who would call sin "an objective and corporate condition of having-gone-wrongness, of having missed the mark, got off-center, which means that man lacks the crowning glory, the true divine humanity, which should be his"[192] It is important to underline that when we speak about sin we must localize it around concrete persons; it is an individual, a particular human being who has chosen against God's goodness out of bad will, laziness or fear, and it is that individual that must accept responsibility for his or her sin in order to seek and find freedom from sin.

Obviously we are caught in this web of sin; it looks like there is no way to escape from it. If we are not dealing with original sin which we inherited from our first parents (Adam and Eve), we find

---

[192] *Francis Pereira, Gripped by God in Christ, P. 73*

ourselves daily making choices against God's goodness and will for us or we are being affected by the sins of others which might include our family, culture or even nation. Sin is a reality in the human exigency that we cannot pretend to ignore; we must face up with it. St. Paul VI (Pope) writing in *AAS* put it so succinctly, "It is human nature so fallen, stripped of grace that clothed it, injured in its own natural powers and subjected to the dominion of death, that is transmitted to all men, and it is in this sense that every man is born in sin"[193] What is our way out? The apostle Paul highlighted the helplessness of the individual before the pull of sin which reveals the contradiction that exists in human nature as he observed, "I can will what is right, but I cannot do it. For I do not do the good I want, but I do the evil I do not want" (Romans 7:18-19). He then delivered his final verdict on the human condition, "Miserable one that I am! Who will deliver me from this mortal body?" (Romans 7:24). The individual who pretended that he was absolute master of himself has finally realized that he needed help. This is the condition of the unredeemed humanity.

Fortunately St. Paul had experienced the saving power of Jesus Christ and was aware of what immense grace was present to humanity through the grace of Christ and so he would then go forward in the verse following (Rom 7:25) to underline the immeasurable help we have received from the coming of Christ and our faith in Him. This is grace. Without the grace of Christ, humanity is hopelessly doomed. As Francis Pereira, SJ observed, "No individual man, nor all men together can free him from this state. Of his own strength man cannot save himself; he cannot break the deadly grip the indwelling sin lays on him"[194] Sin, both as the universal condition of unredeemed

---

[193] *Pope Paul VI, AAS, P.439*
[194] *Francis Pereira, Gripped by God in Christ, P. 72*

humanity and the actual free choice of the individual to revolt against God, has its remedy only in the obedience of Christ. In the twelfth chapter of his letter to the Romans, St. Paul forcefully argues to the fact that the effects of the sin that came into the world through the disobedience of Adam have been remedied by the event of Christ coming into the world. Jerome Murphy O'Connor agrees with St. Paul on this idea in his book, *Sin and Repentance* where he alluded to the fact that: Sin explains everything about Jesus, his teaching, his work, his death on Calvary, his return to heaven, which sin had shut to mankind and which by him and with him opened its gates anew.[195]

Pope St. John Paul II amplified the liberating power of Christ over sin in several of his encyclical letters: In *Reconciliatio et Paenitentia*, he wrote, "we can say that in order not to sin or in order to gain freedom from sin the Christian has within himself the presence of Christ and the mystery of Christ, which is the mystery of God's loving kindness"[196] Elsewhere in the encyclical on the splendor of truth, *'Veritatis Splendor'* he taught, "Christ has redeemed us! This means that he has given us the possibility of realizing the entire truth of our being; he has set our freedom free from the domination of concupiscence".[197] The reality of Christ – his incarnation, passion and resurrection - and our acceptance of him throws a challenge to all Christians today. We must all make a fundamental choice for what is good against what is evil; we must choose truth over lie; light over darkness; freedom over slavery. This is what accords to our freedom in Christ. Being free in Christ, sin cannot be a lifestyle of choice. Sin is an abuse of freedom. According to the apostle Paul, every act of sinfulness is tantamount to slavery and that is why he cautioned the

---

[195] *Jerome Murphy O'Connor, Sin and Repentance, P. 18-21*

[196] *Reconciliatio et Paenitentia, #20*

[197] *Veritatis Splendor, #103*

Christian, "For freedom Christ has set us free; stand fast therefore, and do not submit again to the yoke of slavery" (Galatians 5:1). To stand fast i.e. to live righteously is to live in freedom; it is the antidote to the slavery of sin. The admonition of St. John Paul II comes handy here when he wrote, "Sustained by the mystery of Christ as by an interior source of spiritual energy, the Christian, being a child of God, is warned not to sin and indeed receives the commandment not to sin but to live in a manner worthy of 'the house of God, that is, the church of the living God'"[198]

II.   The Meaning of Suffering

Christians are familiar with a prayer we have all come to know as the Serenity Prayer which goes thus: "God grant me the serenity to accept the things I cannot change; courage to change the things I can; and wisdom to know the difference". For me this prayer encapsulates the thoughts of Viktor Frankl on the question of suffering. In his opinion the cause of our suffering may be beyond us and most often we do not have any way of overcoming the situation. Yet we should not allow the reality of suffering to have the last word, in fact our suffering does not determine who we are, rather our attitude in the face of suffering will reveal the meaning of our lives. It is not about what happens to us, but about our response to the events that occur in our lives that will determine the quality and content of our character. Viktor Frankl counsels us: "For what then matters is to bear witness to the uniquely human potential at its best, which is to transform a personal tragedy into a triumph, to turn one's predicament into a human achievement"[199]

---

[198] *Reconciliatio et Paenitentia, #21*
[199] *Viktor Frankl, Man's Search for Meaning, P. 135*

Viktor Frankl submitted that suffering is not something that one should go out in search of as if it were a good in itself; rather one is only to seek to find meaning out of the unavoidable suffering that befalls one. In his words, "To suffer unnecessarily is masochistic rather than heroic"[200] Interestingly, even though the story of Viktor Frankl especially as a Jew in the days of the Nazi occupation of Eastern Europe is essentially the story of suffering, Viktor didn't seem to have spent time in exposing or dealing with the why of suffering, rather he preoccupied himself with making the best out of the situation one finds oneself, i.e. what can I tell the world about my character as a person in spite of my suffering? Should I get sad and grumpy because of my predicament or is there a possibility that this could become an opportunity for me to reveal the quality of my person as a human being. In other words Viktor Frankl is asking us to see how we can turn our stumbling stone into stepping stone; turn our difficulty into an opportunity. So far so good, but the Christian in me tells me that there is more we can see in our suffering than just opportunities of self-enthronement.

Suffering is related to evil and human beings are constantly asking: why is there evil in the world? In an attempt to find the answer we are obliged to look beyond ourselves. In his encyclical on the Christian meaning of human suffering, St. John Paul II wrote, "For man does not put this question to the world, even though it is from the world that suffering often comes to him, but he puts it to God as the creator and Lord of the world"[201] Unless we see evil and the subsequent suffering that emanates from it through the lenses of faith, we might not be able to find any meaning in suffering. God's answer to the problem of evil and suffering was to show how much he

---

[200] *Ibid. P. 136*

[201] *John Paul II, Salvifici Doloris, P. 13*

loved the world and He sent his only begotten Son, Jesus Christ (Cf. John 3:16) who suffered and died on the cross in order to overcome evil in the world. And St. John Paul II continued, "And even though the victory over sin and death achieved by Christ in His cross and resurrection does not abolish temporal suffering from human life, nor free from suffering the whole historical dimension of human existence, it nevertheless throws a new light upon this dimension and upon every suffering: the light of salvation"[202]

The suffering of Christ, especially since it was the suffering of the innocent on behalf of another (substitutive suffering) reveals to us that suffering is redemptive. This is probably what Viktor was referring to when he said, "In some way, suffering ceases to be suffering at the moment it finds a meaning, such as the meaning of a sacrifice"[203] Suffering becomes meaningful when one is undergoing it out of love for the other; one chooses to suffer rather than allow a loved one go through suffering. This is evident when you see a parent taking care of a sick child, how a parent readily gives up all forms of comfort in order to be with the child and to provide for the child. This is also the case among spouses who would easily take on any difficulty for the sake of the one they love.

Suffering especially when it is accepted valiantly makes us stronger and reveals the best in humanity both in the one who suffers and the individuals who get involved with the sufferer. It enables us to see how much humanity can take and still remain uncontaminated or untarnished by the circumstance that one finds oneself. Suffering tests our character and helps us to put things in perspective. It's like we need some degree of suffering in order to kick start our lives as Ralph Sockman once wrote: "Without danger there would be no

[202] *Ibid. P. 21*
[203] *Viktor Frankl, Man's Search for Meaning, P. 135*

adventure. Without friction our cars would not start and our spirits would not soar. Without tears, eyes would not shine with the richest expressions"[204] If we do not despise suffering for what it looks like to us at the time; if we were to embrace it as part of the human reality, we will eventually find the hidden meaning and be glad that we did. This is the kind of optimism that Viktor Frankl has discovered and encouraged in humanity. We are never to allow our suffering dominate us and induce us into taking a pessimistic approach to life, rather let us open our lives to learning from the school of suffering, the virtues of courage and patience.

Several incidents of people suffering for instance during wars, natural disasters (flood, hurricanes, earthquakes, famine, etc.) or other forms of physical suffering have tended to galvanize the human race as we see the out pouring of concern from all over the world towards the victims. Obviously the milk of human sympathy is not dry yet. It seems like humanity realizes its relatedness more during situations of suffering. In his encyclical letter on the Christian meaning of Suffering, Blessed John Paul II had observed, "People who suffer become similar to one another through the analogy of their situation, the trial of their destiny, or through their need for understanding and care, and perhaps above all through the persistent question of the meaning of suffering"[205]

Suffering also brings out the best in humanity – shows us how much a person can take on behalf of another and the capacity in humanity to empathize with one another. As St. John Paul II observed in his encyclical letter, "Although the world of suffering exists 'in dispersion', at the same time it contains within itself a

---

[204] *Sockman Ralph,* The Meaning of Suffering, *P.66*
[205] *John Paul II, Salvifici Doloris, P.11*

singular challenge to communion and solidarity"[206] Around the world we see how people easily rally around people suffering from wars and natural disasters to provide as much help as possible. People even put themselves through dangers in order to assist. People run into burning houses to try to rescue those trapped by fire, etc. They suffer yes, but they show us the quality of humanity that is not yet destroyed by the evil of hatred, selfishness, greed and envy. Situations of suffering reveal to us that there is still a lot of good left in humanity; it is not all doom and gloom. And this Viktor noticed that not only in the concentration camp, rather "Everywhere man is confronted with fate, with the chance of achieving something through his own suffering".[207]

III.   Freedom from the fear of Death

Death as a topic frequently inspires Poets, Novelists, Philosophers, and especially Theologians today, but it is also a subject which has forced itself upon man's attention from the earliest times of history. In the hours of naked frankness, every thinking person - I as well as others – will be confronted with the problem, or should I rightly say, the mystery. So many of my friends have gone forever! And the fate of those whom I still love is sealed; they too must go someday. Sooner or later my own hour will strike. Such clear evidence no one can completely shroud in the darkness. Much as I may desire to flee from every reminder, and behave as if others only – and none but strangers - are surely to die, I am constantly faced with my own death. A lot of times we ask the question but why must we die? Yet we know as many have already said and John Sachs observed

---

[206] *John Paul II, Salvifici Doloris, P. 11*

[207] *Viktor Frankl, Man's Search for Meaning, P. 89*

in his book, "death is what makes us live with a profound sense of accountability"[208]

Death spies upon, haunts me every day and has its foot at my door, but itself remains no less a terrible secret. The first binding sheet of the dead is silence. Then the body is buried; I mean literally hidden from the rest of humanity. The deceased, left alone becomes so quickly no longer the person I used to know and love. What happens then to the person? Will that body survive in some manner? And what shall become of me? These are questions of prime importance, and such that neither science nor technology of which we are so proud, is equipped enough to answer. In some cases doubtless, we manage to put off the date, i.e. we delay the event, but death itself no one can attempt or hope to destroy. The thought of death fills us with trepidation; we would have loved to wish it away and in fact "we don't like to look death in the face"[209] According to Christoph Schonborn in his book *From Death to Life*, death has been very largely suppressed from our view. He continues by citing Philippe Aries who insisted that "Death has become the most trenchant prohibition of the modern world"[210] Such is humanity's attitude towards death, an attitude from which we must be freed.

Humanity through the ages is interested in seeking freedom from this phenomenon called death. Incidentally most of the effort has been geared towards evading, avoiding and defeating death at all cost. John MacQuarrie has painted a vivid picture of the effort that humanity has continued to make in a bid to escape from the grip of death as he wrote in his book, *An Existential Theology*, "Fallenness is related to the flight from death. In his everyday inauthentic existence

---

[208] *John R. Sachs, The Christian Vision of Humanity, P. 76*
[209] *Ibid. P. 76*
[210] *Christoph Schonborn, From Death to Life, P. 172*

man avoids the thought of death and conceals from himself its real significance. We are all familiar with symptoms of this flight from death. Some people have a horror of cemeteries or even going to see their dying friends and family in the hospital. The very word death is avoided and euphemism substituted for it – 'passing away', 'being at rest' and so on. Since fallen man is concerned with the world and has founded his life on it, to go out of the world means for him the shattering of his existence and he does not wish to think of it. 'People die' – that much is recognized, but in this way death is depersonalized. The impersonal way of speaking serves to conceal the real issue, which is that I die, and that my death is disclosed to me as a present possibility. In everyday conversation on death, it is generalized … and its significance for my existence is evaded"[211] The human person is a being drawn by the need for freedom; and also the need to attain and maintain prosperity, even eternal prosperity. The way I see it, all of the individual's strivings are basically motivated by the desire to escape the burden imposed by the dread of extinction and insignificance. But unfortunately these methods have not given men the freedom they seek.

This would lead one to ask the question, where is the root of this fear of death? Where does death get its sting from? St. Paul makes a bold attempt at an answer to this question when he wrote in 1 Corinthians 15:56, "The sting of death is sin, and the power of sin is the law. But thanks be to God who gives us the victory through our Lord Jesus Christ". I totally agree with the analysis of John Sachs about the relationship between sin, death and fear as he wrote, "To turn away from the Lord is to die, not because the Lord strikes down the sinner, but because the sinner has abandoned the

---

[211] *John MacQuarrie, An Existential Theology, P.119*

only source of real life there is"[212] Elsewhere he would conclude, "Apart from physical pain, perhaps what we fear and humanly suffer in death is radical loneliness, being completely isolated and cut off: not only from our loved ones but most especially from God"[213] As Pannenberg puts it, "death, which is a separation from life, is also, in the proper sense, a radical separation from God"[214]. And this idea of separation from God is indeed a very dreadful one. The Christian doctrine that makes it certain that there will be judgment after death seems to be a huge contributing factor that makes people really afraid of death. Maybe if there was an assurance to individual Christians that they will not be condemned, most likely a lot of people will be begging and running to their deaths just as some of the martyrs of the early Church, such as St. Polycarp, St. Ignatius of Antioch, etc. did. I once read a text attributed to a certain Tsoisfontaines who was a Philosopher- theologian and it said, "In fact there are souls among us – and they are often the best – who are yearning for its arrival, and meet it with joyful rapture. Their body is exhausted, yet they are nearing fulfillment, or so they appear to think. We must not lose sight of this positive aspect of the end".

This then turns our attention to the need to live and die with Christ. Unless our death is seen along the lines of the death of Christ, it is utter destruction and extinction. Pannenberg had followed Karl Rahner in developing this thesis when he interjected, "The only question then is whether in death there is an opening to God as there was in the death of Jesus, or whether on the contrary there is a closing of self to God, so that the death is under the sign of sin".[215]

---

[212] *John R. Sachs, The Christian Vision of Humanity, P.77*
[213] *Ibid. P. 78*
[214] *Wolfhart Pannenberg, Anthropology in Theological Perspective, P. 140*
[215] *Ibid. P. 139*

For Christ his death meant a triumph and glorification as he hung on the cross fulfilling the will of God His Father. His death was not an empty one; it was not the mere dissolution of the body, it was the accomplishment of life's task (John 17:1). Joseph Ratzinger (Pope Emeritus Benedict XVI) saw the various ways in which human beings have attempted to create immortality for themselves, albeit unsuccessfully, and proposed what he thought would be a way out for humanity in the face of the fear of death, "If this is so, then only one could truly give lasting stability: he who is, who does not come into existence and pass away again but abides in the midst of transience: the God of the living, who does not hold just the shadow and echo of my being, whose ideas are not just copies of reality…In him I can stand as more than a shadow; in him I am truly closer to myself than I should be if I just tried to stay by myself"[216] This one that he is proposing is Jesus Christ, the Second Person in the Blessed Trinity. In him is our victory over fear and death.

For Christ, death meant liberation and so should death be for all who live like Christ; His reward will be their reward. For scripture says, "If we have died with Him we shall also live with him; if we persevere we shall also reign with him. But if we deny him he will deny us" (2 Timothy 2:11-12). John R. Sachs aptly captures the picture when he wrote, "To die with Christ is not to be spared suffering, fear or death, but it is to be filled with Christ's own Spirit, and therefore with the same courage that gave him the power and confidence to face the demands of his life and death honestly and willingly[217]. It is our faith in Jesus' victory over sin, death, and the devil that gives us the courage to renounce the fear of death and walk in the power of God's Spirit (see 1 Timothy 1:7). When fear of death

---

[216] *Joseph Cardinal Ratzinger, Introduction to Christianity, PP. 303-304*
[217] *John R. Sachs, The Christian Vision of Humanity, P. 80*

is removed, we are free to live in self-giving love. We no longer need fear the evil powers - sin, death, and the devil - and can now face the future in the resurrection power of God and the hope this brings. The way I see it, life (death) with Christ is an endless hope, while life (death) without Christ is a hopeless end. It is this hopelessness that is frightening in death; it is not really death itself. As philosophers would put it, it is not extinction that people worry about; rather it is extinction with insignificance that they worry about.

Christoph Schonborn cited the work of a fourteenth century theologian, Nicholas Cabasilas (*On Life in Christ*) where he argued on the importance of living with Christ in this world if we are to have victory over death. I have found his words as addressing the fear that we have about death and the hope, promise and freedom that abound if one were to trust in Christ. I would wish to reproduce that interesting portion here: "Life in Christ comes into being in the present life and begins thence. But it is perfected in the coming life, after we have entered that Day. And if it has not already begun here, neither the present existence nor even future existence is able to bestow that life in Christ on the souls of men in its perfected state. For fleshly existence spreads darkness in the present life, and this gloom and transiency cannot inherit imperishability. This is why Paul thought it better to depart and be with Christ, for he says: "it is far better to depart and be with Christ" (Phil. 1:23).... On that Day, his friends are permitted to share with the Son of God in his mysteries, and they are permitted to hear from him what he himself has heard from the Father. But it is only those who are already his friends and have ears that attain to that place. For it is not first there that friendship is made, that the ear is opened, the nuptial garment made ready and all the rest prepared that is fitting for that Bridegroom: no, the present life is the workshop for all of this. And one who does not already possess these things before his decease will have no share in that life"[218] Our fear will be conquered by love – love of Christ who gave his life that we may live.

So far I have highlighted the fear that human beings have of the reality of death, and have argued that the various ways we have tried to cope with this reality especially the attempt to set up immortality symbols including our accomplishments and offspring after us would not be right response to the mystery and fear of death; only faith in Christ assures us of victory over the fear of death. I wish to conclude this discussion with the thoughts of Pope St. John Paul II when he wrote, "This natural aversion to death and this incipient hope of immortality are illumined and brought to fulfillment by Christian faith, which promises and offers a share in the victory of the Risen Christ: it is the victory of the one who, by his redemptive death, has set man free from death, "the wages of sin" (Rom 6:23), and has given him the Spirit, the pledge of resurrection and of life (cf. Rom 8:11). The certainty of future immortality and hope in the promised resurrection cast new light on the mystery of suffering and death, and fill the believer with an extraordinary capacity to trust fully in the plan of God"[219]

IV.   Resurrection of the Body

Resurrection of the body is another way, albeit a deeper way of speaking of the victory over death. In speaking of the resurrection of the body, we are not just recalling the events of the resurrection of Christ which Christians recall every Easter Sunday, rather we are referring to a reality which concerns every believer. In other

---

[218] *Christoph Schonborn, From Death to Life, PP. 186-187*

[219] *John Paul II, Evangelium Vitae, #67*

words, what God has accomplished in His Son, Jesus Christ, He will also do in all those who live and die like Christ, i.e. those who live in obedience to the will of God as Christ did. To speak of the resurrection of the body is our Christian way of affirming the value of the body unlike the doctrines (Gnosticism, Albegianism, etc.) that denigrate the body while exalting the soul as if the body and soul are two distinct components of the human being at war with each other. John Sachs insists and I agree with him that "Body and soul are not composite parts, but different ways of describing the complex living reality of the single, total human person".[220] Particularly in Gnostic thinking, material, including the body, was irrelevant. It is in the light of this that I prefer the wording of the final article of the Apostles' Creed which reads: 'I believe in the resurrection of the body' to the wording of the final article of the Nicene Creed in the new Roman Missal which reads: 'I believe in the resurrection of the dead'. Even today, after the exaltation of St. John Paul II in his audiences between 1979 and 1984, there is a renewed interest in the theology of the body that consistently holds up the body as an essential component in the human person along with the soul and spirit. The body is no longer to be viewed as a component to be conquered and relegated to the background.

It is not as if there was ambiguity in the Church's understanding of the dignity of the body from the beginning, rather the series of heresies she has had to deal with in the past has left its trails and often unsuspecting theologians and church people have picked up some of these distortions and subsequently passed them on unwittingly. There was thinking among Christians that it would make more sense to concentrate on "the salvation of their 'souls', which unlike the mortal

---

[220] John R. Sachs, *The Christian Vision of Humanity*, P. 54

(corruptible) body, could go to heaven"[221] With this development, effectively, a dichotomy has been introduced in the human person between the body and the soul; and definitely, the body came off worse for it. But the truth is, if we serve God here on earth with our bodies and our souls, then it follows that both our bodies and souls will be equally rewarded with resurrection. I mean this is only logical. And it is to this truth that St. Justin Martyr spoke when he taught, "Indeed, God calls even the body to resurrection and promises it everlasting life. When he promises to save the man, he thereby makes his promise to the flesh. What is man but a rational living being composed of soul and body? Is the soul by itself a man? No, it is but the soul of a man. Can the body be called a man? No, it can but be called the body of a man. If, then, neither of these is by itself a man, but that which is composed of the two together is called a man, and if God has called man to life and resurrection, he has called not a part, but the whole, which is the soul and the body" (*The Resurrection* 8 [A.D. 153]).

To have a good understanding of the resurrection of the body, we have to understand better the implication of the resurrection of Jesus Christ from the dead. Samuel Rayan, S.J. discussing the relevance of the person and message of Jesus for our times, expressed the fact that the "Resurrection of Jesus is above all else the revelation and realization of God-with-us, and the token of it is that the presence of Jesus has become interior to our consciousness, interior to our freedom, not doing things for us as we remain passive but empowering us"[222] His Resurrection, just like his Incarnation is God's way of exercising power for our salvation. The Jesus event is God's proximity and the

---

[221] *Ibid. P. 84*

[222] *Samuel Rayan, SJ, Jesus: The relevance of His Person and Message for our Times, P.95*

promise of humanity. It was the body of Jesus that was crucified, died and buried, yet it was that same body that rose from the dead, after all according to the report in John 20:27, "His flesh still bears the marks of the nail"[223] Yes, there were obviously something different about the risen Jesus, which was why he was not immediately recognized by his close friends, yet it was substantially Jesus. As John Sachs captured it, "It is really Jesus, but it is a Jesus transformed, a Jesus who, though bone of our bones and flesh of our flesh, can no longer 'be held' by the world"[224] Just as the body of Jesus experienced resurrection, so will our 'mortal bodies' experience resurrection too. What God has accomplished in His Son, He will also accomplish in us who are His adopted sons and daughters, co-heirs with Jesus (cf. I Corinthians 6:14). In his work on the 'Last Things', Regis Martin highlighted the thoughts of St. Augustine on the issue of the resurrection of the body when he wrote, "Christ realized what is still a hope for us... We are the body of that head in whom what we expect became a reality"[225]

St. Paul, more than any other author in the Scriptures, speaks of the resurrection of the body, indicating that the body will be transformed from corruptibility to incorruptibility (cf. I Corinthians 15:51). In fact he devoted the whole 58 verses of chapter 15 of his first letter to the Corinthians discussing the issue of the resurrection of the body. He also makes the important link between the resurrection of Christ and the value of the human body. For him, "because of the resurrection, the body is 'for the Lord, and the Lord for the body'"[226] If we hope for the resurrection of the body, then we must treat the body with the dignity it deserves while we possess it here and now.

---

[223] *John R. Sachs, The Christian Vision of Humanity, P. 86*

[224] *Ibid. P. 86*

[225] *Regis Martin, The Last Things, P. 22*

[226] *John R. Sachs, The Christian Vision of Humanity, P. 88*

In Christ rising from the dead with his body, a powerful message is sent to the world that nothing created by God, especially the human body could be treated with disdain. At the appointed time God will raise our mortal bodies into glory- this is what St. Paul terms 'the redemption of our bodies' (Romans 8:23). If our souls are to be saved, as we believe it will happen, it is important for us also to realize that it is the totality of the human person, i.e. body, soul and spirit which will be saved. The glorification of a part will invariably mean the glorification of the whole, as John R. Sachs rightly observed, "The fact that human life is real only in the inseparable, irreducible totality of spirituality and corporeal dimensions means that we may not think of our final destiny in terms of souls who have no connection whatsoever to material reality"[227]

V. Freedom in relation to our final destiny and Christian living

In any discussion about our final destiny, our thoughts go right away to what the Church calls the four Last things, which include Death, Judgment, Heaven and Hell. The interesting thing about this discussion is that it is implicit in our Christian life, that is to say, every move I make as a Christian would be guided by questions related to the Last four things: How am I to die a good and holy death? How am I to meet judgment before God? How am I to avoid Hell? How am I to obtain Heaven?[228] Consciousness of these realities (the four last things) will influence the way we live and the choices we make. Actions have consequences; there are certain principles that should guide our actions, realizing that certain choices will lead us to eternal happiness, which is heaven while other choices will lead us to eternal

---

[227] *Ibid. P. 90*

[228] *Regis Martin, The Last Things, P.23*

darkness, which is Hell. It is not as if we can all so well have the situation under our control, it is all dependent on God and how we see and relate to God.

Yes, God is a judge, yet he is above all our Creator and Savior who does not want anyone who believes in Him to perish but to have eternal life (John 3:16). God is love and is prepared to give us as many chances as possible for us to make the right choice. Joseph Ratzinger put it beautifully in his book, *Introduction to Christianity*, when he wrote, "This is the source of a profound freedom, a knowledge of God's unrepentant love; he sees through all our errors and remains well disposed to us"[229] It was to ensure our salvation that God sent His only begotten Son, Jesus Christ, to die on the cross. However, it is important for us to remind ourselves that the final judgment for each individual would be based on the choices the individual has made during life with regard to whether one accepted Jesus or rejected him. Put somewhat differently, we have a judgment to make, which is in the form of the response we give to the offer of salvation made to us by Jesus.

The understanding would be that every individual while on earth is preparing one's own judgment sheet for to paraphrase St. Therese of Lisieux, "One receives as much from God as one hopes for". In every day parlance, this would sound like the expression we hear too often, 'as you make your bed, so shall you lay on it'. In the Scriptures, Jesus constantly reminded us that the way we relate to one another, and especially the way we respond to the needs of the less fortunate members of society will go a long way in helping to fashion the outcome of our judgment on the last day (cf. Matthew 25:31-46). As John Sachs summarized it, "The judgment of God therefore is not a sentence imposed from without. We may think of it as the act

---

[229] *Joseph Ratzinger, Introduction to Christianity, P. 325*

in which God ratifies the judgment we ourselves have made in the concrete choices of our lives"[230] This agrees with the thoughts of Socrates who was quoted as saying that he wanted to live already now in such a way that he can "appear before the judge with a soul as healthy as possible"[231]

Among religions and religious people, talk about heaven and hell is significantly prevalent. Often they are presented as places that individuals would end depending on the judgment made on the last day about the way they lived their lives on earth. But it is essential for us to understand these terms as a state of being; being for God or against God –"God accepted and loved is heaven; God rejected and lost is hell"[232] While the kingdom of heaven refers to being in the presence of God, hell is the construction of a particular individual who refuses the presence of God. Hell is the sinner's rejection of God, not God's rejection of the sinner. In the formulation of Regis Martin, "Hell is a condition or a state of soul where God cannot be found, nor can he find us; where all reassuring lights of faith and hope have gone out"[233] Hell is the highest form of isolation that an individual can impose on oneself, a self- imprisonment, whereby "there is nothing to escape from and nothing to escape to. One is always alone"[234] This is despair, the absence of hope. Authors are indeed unanimous in underlining the fact that hell is a self-inflicted injury on the individual. John Sachs citing Origen wrote, "Each sinner ignites the 'fire' of his or her own hell. Hell is 'in' such a person; people are not 'in' hell"[235] Meanwhile, heaven is the individual's openness to

---

[230] *John R. Sachs, The Christian Vision of Humanity, P. 95*

[231] *Christoph Schonborn, From Death to Life, P.185*

[232] *John R. Sachs, The Christian Vision of Humanity, P.98*

[233] *Regis Martin, The Last Things, P.110*

[234] *T.S. Elliot, The Cocktail Party: A Comedy, P.87*

[235] *John R. Sachs, The Christian Vision of Humanity, P. 99*

receive God's gift of his love and mercy. In other words, heaven is the creation of the gracious God; hell is the product of the perverse and obdurately sinful individual.

The rudimentary catechism I learnt during the religious education classes taught me that God created human beings out of love, so that we may know Him, love Him, serve Him and at last come to be with Him in heaven. Obviously God did not create us for damnation (Hell); He has a plan for us to spend our eternity with Him. In the light of this I am convinced that God has a plan for universal salvation of all his creatures. In the context of our discussion, salvation is another way of speaking of liberation that is synonymous with freedom. In my opinion I believe that optimism of presumption is a better option here than pessimism of despair. I believe that we are saved by the death and glorious resurrection of Christ – by his wounds we have been healed (I Peter 2:24b). However we must remember that we have the obligation to become disciples of Christ, not just his admirers. It is our way of bearing the fruits of the redemption which he wrought for us by his death and resurrection. John R. Sachs reminds us that "Christian discipleship means mission and ministry"[236] We must desire to live out the kingdom values which Jesus lived, preached and died for. Like Christ, we must always be prepared to say, not my will O Lord, but thy will be done. This submission to the will of God is the key to our freedom from all the conditions militating against the full realization of our humanity and indeed our final destiny.

---

[236] *Ibid. 104*

CHAPTER 7

FREEDOM IS AN ALL INCLUSIVE PHENOMENOM

I.   Freedom is found only in relationship with others

John R. Sachs in the first section of his book, *The Christian Vision of Humanity*, articulates very well the human reality- that humanity did not just happen, neither is it purposeless. God, of his own freewill, created humanity so that we could assist him in caring for the earth. Humanity is the most active and visible link in the relationship between God and all his creatures. Contrary to the claims of certain individuals, the earth has not been given to us to harness and even sometimes to exploit as unfortunately is the case when trees are cut down for commercial purposes and not replaced without considering the adverse effect it has on the environment. In fact we are stewards of the earth; "We must learn to see ourselves as gardeners, careful tenders of the earth, realizing that our mutual survival and development is at stake".[237] Wolfhart Pannenberg totally agrees with John Sachs, when citing the work of Thus Altner he wrote, "The mastery of nature to which human beings are called according to the account of

---

[237] *John R. Sachs, The Christian Vision of Humanity, P. 22*

creation in the Priestly document must be exercised in awareness of the creator's own dominion over his creation. This means that human beings have not been given carte blanche for the selfish pillage and exploitation of nonhuman nature.[238]

To better appreciate our lives and that of other creatures, we must understand humanity in an ecological context. This means that "We are not merely beings who walk on the earth, we come from it and are truly a part of it"[239] Whatever concerns we have for ourselves should be equally extended to the rest of God's creatures. This was the position of Peter Singer in his book *Practical Ethics*, where he highlighted the thoughts of two great philosophers/environmentalists Albert Schweitzer and Paul Taylor. First he cited the work of Schweitzer in his well acclaimed doctrine of the universal reverence for life in which he taught, "I am life which wills to live, and I exist in the midst of life which wills to live… Just as in my own will-to-live there is a yearning for more life, and for that mysterious exaltation of the will which is called pleasure, and terror in face of annihilation and that injury to the will-to-live which is called pain; so the same obtains in all the will-to-live around me, equally whether it can express itself to my comprehension or whether it remains unvoiced"[240] Following upon this teaching of Schweitzer, Paul Taylor argued in his book *Respect for Nature* "that every living thing is pursuing its own good in its own unique way. Once we see this, we can see all living things as we see ourselves and therefore we are ready to place the same value on their existence as we do on our own"[241] Recognizing the value of my own life, I should be sincere enough to acknowledge the value of the life

---

[238] *Pannenberg Wolfhart, Anthropology in Theological Perspective, P. 78*

[239] *John R. Sachs, The Christian Vision of Humanity, P. 22*

[240] *Peter Singer, Practical Ethics, P.278*

[241] *Ibid. P.279*

of the other creature and therefore the need to protect it. The 'golden rule' comes alive here when Jesus said to us "Do unto others whatever you would have them to do to you" (Matthew 7:12). If we all treated each other right, if we all respected the dignity of each other, then we would have a world where the lamb can dwell in peace with the lion and the rich would understand their responsibility to the poor. This is very close to the ethics of Albert Schweitzer in the doctrine of universal reverence for life. His was an ethics that recognized our interdependence on one another (and this includes every living creature), as he would insist, "In the very fibers of our being, we bear within ourselves the fact of the solidarity of life"[242]

We so desire life and freedom, which is a very good thing, but we must realize that it is not just human beings that desire and deserve to live and experience freedom; all of God's creation yearns for life and we are called upon to join with God in the preservation of the life of the world. What we do in enhancing the earth contributes immensely to the quality of our lives as human beings, as John R. Sachs observes, "The dignity of human beings is especially evident in their partnership with God in caring for creation"[243] In essence, even though we obviously owe our existence to God, it is also important that we understand that we need to nurture a healthy relationship with the rest of God's creation in order to enjoy life in its fullness. Emil Brunner in supporting the stand of Albert Schweitzer on the issue of the universal reverence for life wrote, "...We feel it is displeasing to God deliberately to spoil a tree or a flower. The dumb creatures have a share in the inviolable character of human life. Hence Albert Schweitzer's protest against the current ethic, 'in which

---

[242] *John H. Morgan – Naturally Good, P. 176*
[243] *John R. Sachs, The Christian Vision of Humanity, P. 24*

no animals are allowed to run about', is certainly justified".[244] We do not therefore relate to others or other forms of creation out of sympathy, but rather out of necessity for our own well-being. The good we do for others, we do for ourselves equally.

John Sachs observed that God created humanity to be free when he wrote, "According to the Scriptures, in creating the world out of love in order to be its lover, God made a partner not a puppet"[245] God left humanity with responsibility for what he will become. However this freedom is not a license for one to do whatever one liked, rather it is the capacity to make choice, of course making the right choices as St. John Paul II once said: "Freedom consists not in doing what we like, but in having the right to do what is right".[246]

In his freedom one ought to put everything into the right context, understand the interrelationship between the individual, society, the rest of creation and the Creator. Freedom enables one to recognize one's responsibility in exercising one's freedom for his ultimate happiness, realizing that freedom is at its best when it helps one to be more connected with God and others in society. One who operates from this concept of freedom does not glory in disharmony and divisions; rather he is generous, truthful, just, loving and humble. It is obvious that the most important thing for this kind of freedom is increase in virtue and a never ending aspiration towards the good.

There is a deep yearning in every individual which can only be satisfied by one being in touch with the source and summit of one's life, i.e. God; no wonder St. Augustine had pointed out in 'his

---

[244] *Ara Paul Barsam – Reverence for Life, P. 32.*

[245] *John R. Sachs, The Christian Vision of Humanity P. 28*

[246] *Homily of his holiness John Paul II Oriole Park at Camden Yards, Baltimore Sunday, 8 October 1995*

Confessions' that our hearts have been made for God and we are restless until we rest in God[247] A man is truly free and happy when he submits his will to God. I cannot help but think about what happened in the Garden of Eden according to the account in Genesis chapter 3 when Adam and Eve chose to exercise their perceived freedom irrespective of the will of God. What level of unhappiness, shame and discomfort it brought to them, and eventually to the whole of humanity, until the obedience of Jesus changed all that. That goes to show what can happen when we choose against God in the name of freedom.

II. No man is an island

When John Donne, several years ago made the assertion that 'no man is an island', he encapsulated an undisputed reality that has stood the test of time. But yet there are various ways of reading that assertion and applying it. Before the modern age, this notion was stretched to mean that the individual had no freedom and was simply part of a society and one had to adapt to the thinking of the Society to which one found oneself. In those days society determined for the individual what his role was and the emphasis on extended kinship of the entire human race was strong. To a certain extent this was good for human coexistence, but as is true with every system, it had its limits and down side. It ultimately reduced or mitigated individual responsibility and meant that a whole generation or even generations after could be held responsible for the misdeeds of a member of the family. At this point it is obvious that we need a new way of understanding the notion that "no man is an island".

---

[247] *St. Augustine, Confessions, Trans with intro by R.S. Pine, pub By Penguin Books, page 21.*

In today's world, with the spread of Christianity, the axiom is "to be is to be in relation with". As John Sachs puts it, "Life is found only in relationships with others. To be alone is to die"[248] Elsewhere Sachs reminds us that "The cries of the baby remind us that the earliest and abiding experience of personal reality is that I need you to be and become myself"[249] In other words we need others to survive; we are dependent on each other in this world. The neighbor which both the Old Testament and New Testament talked about has become a prominent factor in the life of the individual. The relationship I build with my neighbor will go a long way in determining who I am as an individual. In his theory of the self, George Herbert Mead, an American philosopher and psychologist, had concluded, "The self... is essentially a social structure, and it arises in social experience".[250] The implication is that the individual can only find his being only in a community. The community is the place where life and love are nurtured; it is a place where the individual is helped to develop the right conscience and learn to share of oneself for the good of all. In Christian parlance, the community is the place where the kingdom values of justice, peace, forgiveness, freedom and love are preached and lived. It is contrary to the notion of every one to himself/herself. In all these, the individual appreciates his freedom and understands that freedom is to be used to enhance relationship with others in the community rather than just doing what one wants.

Accepting community as the proper milieu in which one should live out one's humanity and freedom means that one recognizes the equality of all human persons in their dignity as individuals. There is the need for one to recognize that it is human nature, not

---

[248] *John Sachs, The Christian Vision of Humanity – P.31*
[249] *Ibid. P. 36*
[250] *Wolfhart Pannenberg, Anthropology in Theological Perspective, P.185*

gender, race or color that binds us together. Yes those differences are there (actually they constitute what we know as diversity), but the common trait we share as human beings far outweighs the limits that the differences impose on us. Valerie Saiving, a Christian Anthropologist had articulated the issue well when she wrote, "Christian faith and theology rightly consider all human beings as finite, embodied, spiritual, free, sinful, graced and redeemed, but how that is experienced and what it means for women may be quite different than for men"[251] We are in it together and the issue is for each to help the other along the way. We are invited to accept and love the other, not because they are white or black, male or female, tall or short, but simply because they are human beings. In the words of John Sachs, "Male or female, homosexual or heterosexual, single, married or celibate, the real test is whether or not we desire and love others in their real otherness, or whether we only want to take possession of them or try to make them extensions of ourselves".[252] We are encouraged to stop focusing on the dividing lines and instead appreciate the lines that link us together as the human race. This attitude means that we will work as hard for the freedom of every creature as we will work for our own individual freedom.

III. Freedom is the Essence of Existence

At each bend in life, at every particular situation, it seems that the question posed to every individual is simply this: What is the meaning of my life here and now? There is no objective answer to this question, each person has the responsibility to dig in and find the answer for himself/herself. It will definitely vary from individual

---

[251] *John Sachs, The Christian Vision of Humanity – P.46*
[252] *Ibid. P. 49*

to individual, but the point is that it will be particular for each individual. Yet it is not as if to say that the answer is within the individual, but the individual has the responsibility to look around in order to find the meaning. Viktor Frankl identifies this as one of the purposes of his psychotherapeutical method known as Logotherapy – to help the individual rise up to his responsibility. He identified the role of the Logotherapist as "widening and broadening the visual field of the patient so that the whole spectrum of potential meaning becomes conscious and visible to him"[253] In a way this is akin to Socrates viewing his philosophical model as the role of a midwife assisting the process of giving birth to a baby, but in his case giving birth to a thought.

Interestingly, one would only discover or using Viktor's word, actualize oneself only by transcending himself: "In other words, self-actualization is possible only as a side effect of self-transcendence"[254] It is like Christianity would teach that we can only find ourselves in losing ourselves in and for Jesus (Mt. 10:39). However while Viktor thinks of it as a side-effect, Christianity teaches that one should consciously choose this route as the only way to self-actualization. I can only actualize myself by looking beyond myself, looking out for the good of others and being of service to my brothers and sisters. One's fulfillment does not depend on how much one has but rather on how many people one serves. As Dr. Morgan pointed out in his book quoting Albert Schweitzer, "The only ones among you who will be really happy are those who have sought and found how to serve"[255] The relationships I form with the rest of humanity will go a long way in revealing the meaning of my life to me. It is a common

---

[253] *Viktor Frankl, Man's Search for Meaning, P. 132*
[254] *Ibid. P. 133*
[255] *John H. Morgan, Naturally Good, P. 153*

philosophical axiom that to be is to be in relationship with another. No man is an island, so said John Donne several years ago. This is still true even today- to acknowledge the interrelationship between human beings and indeed all of God's creation is essential in one actualizing oneself.

Speaking about relationship and its role in identifying the meaning of one's life, it is important for me as a Christian to recognize that there is both vertical and horizontal relationship which must be observed by the individual if one is to fully realize oneself. By this I mean that one should realize that one has to be in relationship with both God and the rest of creation. Viktor Frankl also captures this when he wrote, "There are people, however, who do not interpret their own lives merely in terms of a task assigned to them but also in terms of the task master who has assigned it to them"[256] Let me say right away that what (who) he calls the task master I understand to mean the Creator who brought humanity into existence and assigned each individual his/her role in the stewardship of all God's creation. We are no accidents, we were created for a purpose; our lives have meaning, and each individual has to find out for himself/herself why they are at a particular place and at a particular time. Why am I here and not there? What am I called to do here? There lies the meaning of my life. This is an unavoidable question to every right thinking individual, and a question one must do well to answer for his/her own sanity and the good of the entire human race. It is the responsibility of the individual and no one can answer it in his place. To rise to the occasion brings fulfillment and self-actualization; to act irresponsibly, i.e. to not play my part adequately will lead to frustration and a feeling of utter meaninglessness of life.

---

[256] *Viktor Frankl, Man's Search for Meaning, P. 132*

IV. Freedom calls us to a reverence for all life

The usual reading of the creation account in the first chapter of Genesis is that the universe and all it contains was created for man's use and pleasure. This is an anthropocentric understanding which places human beings at the center of the universe, but Schweitzer and a lot of other theologians and thinkers, both before and after him, submit that this understanding must change if we are to be fair to the Creator. According to Schweitzer "… we must not place man in the center of the universe"[257]. Elsewhere he observed, "Indeed, when we consider the immensity of the universe, we must confess that man is insignificant"[258] Yes human beings have a special role to play in sustaining creation, i.e. as stewards of creation or may be call them moral agents, but the world does not belong to us. The world belongs to God, an idea that John Burnaby and James Gustafson amplified when they submitted that "all life, the whole universe, exists principally not for humans' wants but for 'the glory of God'"[259]

God had a plan for every creature that he made and invested a value on every creature, human and non-human alike; nothing has he created in vain. In the existence of all these creatures the glory of God is made manifest. God is concerned for every creature, his love and care is boundless, consequently human beings who claim to have been created in the image and likeness of God must have the same boundless care for all of creation, an observation Schweitzer already made: "the boundaries of our moral concern should not be limited to humans in so far as God's purpose extends to the whole of creation"[260]

---

[257] *Ara Paul Barsam – Reverence for Life, P. 147*

[258] *John H. Morgan – Naturally Good, P. 165*

[259] *Ara Paul Barsam – Reverence for Life P.148*

[260] *Ibid. 149*

The position of Schweitzer on the equal value of every creature, even if we will find eventually how difficult it is to carry it through, is an interesting one and like most of his ethics has a Christian underpinning. In the scriptures Jesus speaks about how his heavenly Father cares for both the birds of the air and the flowers in the bush (Matthew 6:26-31). We are also aware (those of us who read the Bible) that during the great flood in the days of Noah, God also saved a pair of every living creature that he has made (Genesis 6:19-22), an indication that their lives are valued equally just as that of humans. Interestingly God put the responsibility on Noah to make provisions for all these creatures; so does God place the responsibility on human beings today to take care of all living creatures. In this Schweitzer was on point and so many theologians and environmentalists would agree with him. Before God every creature has value and God cares for them. He did not create these creatures to abandon them to whims and caprices of humans to determine if they have value or not, and to decide whether they should live or not. Just as human persons fully alive gives glory to God (St. Irenaeus), so does every creature fully alive give glory to God, therefore Schweitzer counsels us: "we are to conduct life so as to relate to all things in a manner appropriate to their relations to God"[261] Unfortunately we live in our own world and so often are not able to articulate how the life of non-human creatures give glory to God.

The mystery of life is too profound for us as humans to fully understand; so any full understanding of the value of each life around us can only be grasped by serving the one who is the principal source of all life i.e. God. Immanuel Kant articulated this idea well when he reasoned along the lines of Schweitzer's idea that "Only by serving every kind of life do I enter the service of that Creative Will whence

---

[261] *Ibid. P. 149*

all life emanates. I do not understand it; but I do know (and it is sufficient to live by) that by serving life, I serve the Creative Will"[262] For us to fully understand the value of every creature, we have to look at them through the eyes of their maker; then shall we see that we are all invested with specific value right from the beginning, and that we are interdependent on one another – human and non-human alike. It's in the light of this that Schweitzer insisted that it was wrong for us to look upon ourselves (human beings) as lord and master over other creatures; if there is one thing we should agree on, it is the fact that we all have one Lord and Master and he is the Creator.

Reverence for life finds a solid base in a theocentric ethic as opposed to a utilitarian ethic in which each creature is looking out for himself and asking what value is the other creature to me or how can I use the other creature for my benefit. Theocentric ethics raises the bar, it calls for a universal respect for every creature and deals a big blow to the selfishness of human persons. Scholars who saw through the lenses of Schweitzer, including Jürgen Moltmann and Hans Kung wisely admonish us: "We should respect the earth, plants and animals for themselves, before weighing up their utility for human beings"[263] If humans want to be counted as truly free, then they must show it by their willingness to serve the least among all God's creature, including animal and plant lives; for our greatness is not measured by how many creatures serve us, but by the number of creatures we serve. Only the truly free individual will recognize the value of every living creature – plant as well as animals. The genius of Schweitzer lies in the fact that he was able to bring us to focus on the big picture – the purpose of the Creator in creation, and to see truly

---

[262] *John H. Morgan – Naturally Good, P. 173*
[263] *Ara Paul Barsam – Reverence for Life, P. 150*

what our position is in creation – that creatures were not created for us, but that we all (human and non-human) were created for 'God's glory'. In our reverence for God is our freedom; and to revere God is to have reverence for all life that God has made.

BIBLIOGRAPHY

Allen James, *As A Man Thinketh*, The Tarcher Family Inspirational Library, New York, 2006.

Ara Paul Barsam, *Reverence for Life – Albert Schweitzer's Great Contribution to Ethical Thought*, Oxford University Press Inc. New York, 2008

Bonevac, Daniel, *Today's Moral Issues: Classic and Contemporary Perspectives*, published by Library of Congress Cataloging –in – Publication Data, 2005

Catechism of the Catholic Church, Liguori Publications, 1994

Fish, S., *There's No Such Thing as Free Speech...and it's a good thing too*, New York: Oxford University Press, 1994.

Frankl, Viktor E., *Man's Search for Meaning*, Washington Square Press, 1985

Gerassi, John. *Jean-Paul Sartre: Hated conscience of his century*. Chicago: University of Chicago Press, 1989.

Hardon, John S.J, *History and Theology of Grace*, Sapientia Press of Ave Maria University, Florida, 2002

Henri De Lubac, *The Mystery of the Supernatural*, Crossroad Publishing Company, New York, 2012

John Paul II, *Evangelium Vitae*, St. Paul Books & Media, Boston MA, 1995

John Paul II, *Reconciliatio et Paenitentia*, St. Paul Books & Media, Boston MA, 1984.

John Paul II, *Salvifici Doloris*, St. Paul Books & Media, Boston MA, 1984

John Paul II, *Veritatis Splendor*, St. Paul Books & Media, Boston MA, 1993.

Joint Declaration on the Doctrine of Justification, William B. Eerdmans Publishing Company, Grand Rapids, Michigan, 2000

Joseph Cardinal Ratzinger, *Introduction to Christianity*, Ignatius Press San Francisco, 2004

Kelley, John Norman Davidson, *Early Christian Doctrines*, London: Adam & Charles Black, 1968.

MacQuarrie, John, *An Existentialist Theology: A Comparison of Heidegger and Bultmann* published by Harper Torchbooks, 1965.

Marnion, Declan & Hines, Mary E., *The Cambridge Companion to Karl Rahner*, Cambridge University Press, New York 2005.

Martin, Regis, *The Last Things*, Ignatius Press San Francisco, 1998

Metz, Johannes B., *Moral Evil Under Challenge*, Herder and Herder, New York, 1970

Mill, J.S., *On Liberty*, Indianapolis: Hackett Publishing, 1978.

Morgan, John H., *Naturally Good*, published by Cloverdale Books, South Bend Indiana, 2005

Murray, Andrew. *The New Life*, published by Destiny Image, 2007.

Odozor, P.I, *Moral Theology in an age of Renewal*, University of Notre Dame, 2003,

O'Connor, Jerome Murphy. *Sin and Repentance*, edited by Dennis O'Callaghan, 1967.

Pazhayampallil Thomas, S.D.B., *Pastoral Guide, Volume 1*, K.J.C Publications, Bangalore India, 1984

Pereira, Francis, S.J., *Gripped by God in Christ*, Printed by Dominic V at St. Paul Press Training School, Bandra, Mumbai, 2005

Pinckaers, Servais, OP, *The Sources of Christian Ethics*, Catholic University of America Press, Washington D.C, 1995

Sachs, John R., *The Christian Vision of Humanity*, published by Liturgical Press, Collegeville, Minnesota, 1991

Samuel Rayan, SJ, *Jesus: The Relevance of His Person and Message for our Times*, edited by Kurien Kunnumpuram, SJ, Bandra Mumbai, 2011

Sartre, Jean Paul., *Being and Nothingness* Printed by First Washington Square Press, 1992

Sartre, Jean Paul., *Existentialism and Human Emotions* published by Kensington Publishing Press New York, 1987

Schubert Ogden, *The Point of Christology* Published by Southern Methodist Press, Dallas, TX, 1992

Schonborn, Christoph, *From Death to Life*, published by Ignatius Press San Francisco, 1995

Singer, Peter, *Practical Ethics* published by Cambridge University Press, New York, 1993

Sockman Ralph, *The Meaning of Suffering*, published by Woman's Division of Christian Service, Board of Missions, Methodist Church, New York, NY, 1961.

St. Augustine, *Confessions*, Trans with intro by R.S. Pine, pub By Penguin Books, London, 1961

St. Augustine of Hippo, *On the Grace of Christ and Original Sin*, Translated by Peter Holmes and Robert Ernest Wallis, and revised by Benjamin B. Warfield. From Nicene and Post-Nicene Fathers, First Series, Vol. 5. Edited by Philip Schaff. Buffalo, NY: Christian Literature Publishing Co., 1887.

Tallentyre, S.G. *The Friends of Voltaire* Published by Cornell University Library, 2009

Tillich, Paul, *The Courage To Be*, printed by Yale University Press, New Haven, CT 1966

Vatican Council II, Conciliar Documents ed. Austin Flannery, O.P., 1982

Wojtyla, Karol. *Love and Responsibility* published by Ignatius Press San Francisco, 1993

Glossary of Terms

AAS- Pope Paul VI, *Acta Apostolicae Sedis*, LX (1968), The Pope Speaks.

Dignitatis Humanae – Vatican II document on the Declaration on Religious Liberty (Dec. 7, 1965)

Evangelium Vitae – Encyclical letter of Pope John Paul II on the Gospel of Life (March 25, 1995)

Reconciliatio et Paenitentia – Post Synodal Apostolic Exhortation of Pope John Paul II on Reconciliation and Penance (In the Mission of the Church Today), (Dec. 2, 1984)

Salvifici Doloris – An Apostolic letter of Pope John Paul II on The Christian Meaning of Human Suffering, (February 11, 1984)

Veritatis Splendor – Encyclical letter of Pope John Paul II on The Splendor of the Truth (August 6, 1993)'

Printed in the United States
By Bookmasters